Turn
Three Shots
into Two

Turn
Three Shots
into Two

*How to Putt, Chip, Pitch, and
Blast Your Way to Lower Scores*

Bill Moretti

with Mike Stachura

**Andrews McMeel
Publishing**

Kansas City

02 03 04 05 06 RDH 10 9 8 7 6 5 4 3 2 1

ISBN: 0-7407-1906-8

Library of Congress Cataloging-in-Publication Data on file.

BOOK DESIGN AND COMPOSITION BY KELLY & COMPANY

To my parents, William and Catherine Moretti;
my wife, Marilyn; and all golf instructors
who share in my passion and devotion
to help others play better golf.

Contents

Acknowledgments

▼ ▼ ▼ ▼

I would like to take this opportunity to thank the following people who have made it possible for me to pursue my golf career:

To my mother and father, Catherine and William Moretti Sr., who gave me their love and provided me with the necessary resources to play and study golf.

To Barry Brown and Steve Shrader, two great friends and golfing companions who helped me through my youth and helped me overcome many obstacles that I have encountered throughout my life.

To Mike Adams for giving me confidence in my ability to teach golf.

To Elmer Schlein, who has been a mentor and a guide through life.

To Julius Germano for being a great help to me in marketing and promoting our golf schools and for the friendship we share.

To Father Laurence Connelly, who has given me spiritual guidance.

To Joe Daleo for supporting me and our golf schools over the years and for his friendship.

To my staff, who give our students, and me, 100 percent every day. With their help, we improve our teaching methods continually.

To all of the students who have attended our golf schools, I thank each and every one of you for your support; it has been a privilege and a joy to help improve your golf games.

Finally, to my wife, Marilyn. I could not ask for a better companion and life mate. She has given of herself unselfishly to support me in my teaching pursuits.

INTRODUCTION

▼ ▼ ▼ ▼

The Value of a
Good Short Game

It could be any Friday afternoon of the golf season on the PGA Tour. The action and mood are typical. Players jockeying for the lead, players scrambling to make the cut, players simply finishing off the day. Nothing especially at stake, perhaps, but then again, because this is the PGA Tour and the scores are there for all the world to see, for these players everything is at stake.

The mind-set for many of the best golfers in the world who earn their living playing golf is a simple, unforgiving, relentless one—namely, you are your number. What you shoot and how you finish says a lot about how you are going to feel. At least for a little while. That is why this game is so appealing. Because even when the stakes are relatively low, the challenge, the intensity, remain high.

And so, as you, the golf fan, sit in your den and watch the proceedings, pay attention to what you're watching, and you'll learn a very important lesson about golf and the business of scoring. At any 30-second point in the day's broadcast, you are very likely to see the following sequence: First, there's Player A facing a testy little pitch from thick greenside rough to a pin just a few paces from the edge of the green. Meanwhile, Player B is studying a 60-foot putt that he must get close to the hole if he's going to save a stroke or two. And then there's Player C, who finds his ball just short of the green in the fairway with a long, uphill chip shot that he, too, must find a way to get up and down. The result in every case is the same. Each man manages to get up and down. He takes two shots instead of three, and he avoids another stumble that might have ruined his day's play. Does it happen this way every time? Clearly not. But it happens enough to make the difference between a score that's over par and one that's under par.

And that's where *your* scoring is going to improve, too. That's the lesson available every week on your television set. It's not very elaborate, but it's a mantra you should begin to know as well as your own name: Scoring in golf begins and ends with the short game.

It is not always the most glamorous part of the game, not the kind of thing that draws oohs and ahs from the fans the way blasting tee shots with incredible distance naturally does. Watch a group of golf fans head over to one of the expansive practice areas you see at pro tournaments. Do you think the first move they make is to check out how Player A is working on his short game? How much time do you think those fans would devote to watching Player B monotonously hit 10, 20, or even 50 four-foot putts in a row? Do you think they'd be excited to watch Player C perfecting his long bunker-shot technique? Odds are, they'd probably walk right by that short-game area as if it were a spot where some maintenance workers were trimming some shrubbery.

It's the long ball that gets everybody excited. Still, while Tiger Woods draws a lot of attention for his long drives, it's the little shots he can hit around and on the greens that have propelled him to most of his victories. The guy who knows how to get the ball in the hole is the one who will be the most formidable competitor and the most successful player. That's a fact in every level of golf. The old saying "You drive for show and you putt for dough" isn't just a catchy phrase. It has real weight to it. Let's look at an example. If you look at the Top 10 players in driving distance in 2000 on the PGA Tour and compare their earnings with those ranked in the Top 10 in putting, I think the evidence will be pretty compelling.

Top 10 in Driving Distance and Earnings

1	John Daly	301.4 yards	$115,460
2	Tiger Woods	298.0 yards	$9,188,321
T3	Davis Love III	288.7 yards	$2,337,765
T3	Phil Mickelson	288.7 yards	$4,746,457
5	Scott McCarron	288.5 yards	$495,975
6	Casey Martin	288.3 yards	$143,248
7	Harrison Frazar	287.3 yards	$608,535
8	Stuart Appleby	286.4 yards	$1,642,221
9	Mathew Goggin	286.3 yards	$414,123
10	Robert Allenby	285.8 yards	$1,968,685
		TOTAL	$21,660,790

Top 10 in Putting Average and Earnings

1	Brad Faxon	1.704*	$999,460
2	Tiger Woods	1.717	$9,188,321
3	Phil Mickelson	1.726	$4,746,457
T4	Paul Azinger	1.733	$1,597,139
T4	Sergio Garcia	1.733	$1,054,338
6	Scott McCarron	1.735	$495,975
7	Skip Kendall	1.738	$947,118
8	Mike Weir	1.740	$2,547,829
T9	Glen Day	1.742	$617,242
T9	Jesper Parnevik	1.742	$2,413,345
		TOTAL	$24,607,224

*putts per green hit in regulation

Clearly, when it comes to the bottom line, being able to putt well was worth about $3 million more than being able to hit it far. In short, good putters make more money. The difference is even more striking when you toss out the three players who ranked in the Top 10 in both driving distance and putting average. The other seven players who were the best putters earned 40 percent more than the seven players who were the longest drivers.

Still not convinced that the short game is where it's at? Then maybe it's worth looking at another chart. This time we'll compare the numbers for two highly different categories: ball striking (which measures how well a player hits fairways and greens) and scrambling (the tour statistic that calculates how often a player is able to make par or better when he misses a green). Now, if you're honest with yourself, you would have to admit that you think the most intriguing thing about pro golfers is how well they hit the ball, in short how great their full swings are. Theoretically, then, the players who have the best full swings should be winning the most money on tour. This is not exactly the case. Let's look at some numbers from late in the 2001 season on the PGA Tour. Here is a comparison of earnings between the best ball strikers and the best scramblers:

Top 8 in Ball Striking

1	Charles Howell III	$1,423,596
2	Joe Durant	$2,245,017
3	Donnie Hammond	$152,698
4	Kenny Perry	$1,555,601
5	J. J. Henry	$994,243
6	Hal Sutton	$1,640,946
7	Tom Lehman	$1,733,926
8	Phil Mickelson	$4,403,883
	TOTAL	$14,149,910

Top 8 in Scrambling

1	Tiger Woods	$5,517,777
2	Nick Price	$1,122,422
3	Scott Hoch	$2,794,319
4	Bob Estes	$2,431,610
5	Mark Brooks	$886,578
6	Davis Love III	$2,558,263
7	Jim Furyk	$2,374,067
8	Bernhard Langer	$1,659,399
	TOTAL	$19,344,435

Surprise, ball striking might be rewarding for some, but it's no financial match for having a good short game.

There's one other statistic that really shows you how important a good short game can be. Of players who finished the year 2000 ranked in the Top 10 in scoring average, nine of them averaged getting up and down better than 60 percent of the time. Eight of the players with the best scoring averages ranked in the top 20 percent on tour in getting up and down. As has been said before, scoring is all about the short game.

Among all PGA Tour players, the average percentage of greens hit in regulation per round is about 65 percent, or 11 or 12 greens per 18 holes. That means they're missing about a third of the greens in regulation per round. But guess what? The scoring average for all players on tour isn't six or seven over par just because they miss six or seven greens around. Not at all. The scoring average on tour is about a stroke *under* par. That says one thing to me: Players' short games are so good that missing a green in regulation does not have to result in an extra stroke automatically being added to their scores. More often than not, there is no bad final result from a poorly executed approach shot. This is because players at the highest level know that if you're going to have a chance to shoot your lowest scores, you're going to have to get good in the short shots. You should know that, too.

Golf is a lot of things to a lot of different people. For some it may be an opportunity to be outdoors on a pretty day. For others it may be a chance to socialize. For most of us it is a challenge that never lets up. But truth be told, when it comes right down to it, most of us who play golf have the same attitude toward the game, be he or she a proven major champion several times over or a rank beginner trying to get around 18 holes for the first time: All of us can get very concerned about our score. After all, that is how we measure up against others, and, more important, against ourselves and our potential. Golf is all about scoring. Everybody thinks about score at some point during their golfing day. In fact, most of us often walk off the 18th green with at least a little irritation over all those extra shots we needlessly added to our total score. And of course, the one place we tend to do the most damage to our scores is around and on the greens. Three putts. Skulled bunker shots. Chunked pitch shots and flubbed chips. These sorts of mistakes seem almost insulting. They are golf's equivalent of what tennis players often call "unforced errors."

The short game may be the most frustrating aspect of golf. The fact that a six-inch putt counts as much as a 300-yard drive almost seems absurd when you think about it a little bit. But I think that's the beauty of the game. In golf, the difficulty and importance of any shot isn't restricted by the distance you have to hit it. In fact, in a way short-game shots are so monumentally important to our scores precisely *because* they are so close to the hole. The object is to get the ball in the hole in as few strokes as possible. When the hole gets close enough to see, it seems we ought at that point to be able to get the ball in the hole. But all too often we take three shots or four when we should be finding a way to make it in two. Just as the pros do on our television sets every week, we can decrease the chance of bad things happening to our score by developing a sound short game. The legendary Bobby Jones said it long ago, and it hasn't changed. "The secret to golf is the ability to turn three shots into two." In the very simplest of terms, all golfers, regardless of how far they hit the ball off the tee or how solidly they hit their irons, should be able to find a way to save a shot or two around the greens whenever possible. Do that often enough and you will be on your way to serious improvement. That is the aim of this book.

The short game comprises four distinct but very much related elements: putting, chipping, pitching, and bunker play. Each element flows from the other, and together they can be the foundation for better scores.

You need to understand that in putting, the simpler your motion, the more reliable it will be. There are tricks to make your stroke easier, and because each person will have his own idiosyncrasies, there are adjustments you can make to get yourself into the habit of rolling the ball correctly, not merely hitting a ball toward the hole. You can also pay attention to your equipment, and change it to better suit your style of putting. In addition, there are a handful of drills that will improve the consistency of your stroke.

In Chapter 2, on chipping, we will show you a method you may have not considered before but one whose simplicity could dramatically improve your distance and direction control. A chipping stroke that is based on your putting motion will be more reliable, especially when the heat is on.

Confidently executed pitch shots can be real stroke savers. In the section on pitching, you will learn the value of balance, rhythm, and consistent club-head speed in getting your shots to travel on the right trajectory that will get the ball to settle around the hole.

Finally, it's time to take the mystery and fear out of bunker shots. There's no reason any average player who pays attention to the simple pre-shot rules of setup and alignment won't be able to develop a motion that will get a ball out of the bunker and onto the green.

Ultimately, the short game is a numbers game. The key is to make the numbers work in your favor. Always take the simplest approach possible. That means putt the ball whenever you can. If ground conditions warrant getting the ball slightly airborne, then chip it. Finally, if you have to get the ball in the air and over a hazard or bunker or mound of one kind or another, then and only then resort to your pitching stroke. Practice your technique with the intention of becoming not merely competent, but confident and comfortable, too. Success in the short game, and in all of golf, comes from having a solid foundation and faith in your abilities. Worry and uncertainty only make it that much more difficult to execute short-game shots well. You can eliminate those shaky feelings through practice.

And there's one other vital way in which you will benefit from a solid short game. If you are a good putter, chipper, pitcher, and bunker player, that knowledge will filter back to your long game. Knowing you are adept at short-game shots, you won't feel pressure to stick every iron close to the hole. Your swing from the fairway will be free-flowing and natural, which is precisely the way you need to swing to be most successful.

Bobby Jones's landmark collection of golf instruction essays, *Down the Fairway,* contains some remarkable insights on the short game. In that book, he writes, "I think it is safe to say that the man who scores between 95 and 100 usually loses about ten strokes per round because of his failure to recover as well as he ought to, even in proportion to his limited ability. Tension, uncertainty and fear take from him a heavier toll than they have any right to exact. . . . Most who play regularly manage somehow to get the ball within short pitching distance of the greens in two shots. It is only then that they really begin to throw away strokes. . . . The short shots ought logically to be the easiest to play; in fact they are, if the player can only keep relaxed. The mechanics are simpler, and the effort considerably less; but the closer one gets to the green, or to the hole, the more difficult it becomes to keep on swinging the club. Those who have no trouble lashing out at a full drive with a fine free swing tighten up in every muscle when confronting a pitch of twenty yards."

Pay attention to these pages and maybe we'll do something about that tension, uncertainty, and fear. Maybe we'll turn them into confidence, conviction, and calm. And that could go a long way toward turning three shots into two.

CHAPTER ONE

PUTTING

▼ ▼ ▼ ▼

Even Ben Hogan Had to Putt

It is perhaps the most famous golf photograph ever taken of one of the most momentous golf shots ever hit: the effortless balance of the legendary Ben Hogan's classic finish, framed by the venerable setting of the 18th hole at Merion Golf Club's famed East Course, outside Philadelphia. Hogan came to this brutish final hole of the 1950 U.S. Open needing a par to force a playoff. With a one-iron in his hand and some 210 yards from the green, Hogan laced a laser of a golf shot toward the green. The ball never wavered from its target, landing gently and settling into the middle of the green. It was a perfect picture of a perfect swing and a perfect shot.

As you'll remember, Hogan made his par after that momentous shot and went on to dominate the playoff the next day over Lloyd Mangrum and George Fazio.

Lovely story. What does it have to do with putting? Well, consider this: Hogan's majestic shot may have reached the green, but it left him no easy two-putt for par. His ball finished some 40 feet away from the hole, a curling uphill putt standing between him and a heroic finish. While Hogan's shot has been the stuff of legend over the years, and while it was a tremendous effort under the circumstances, the job was anything but finished after that swing from the fairway. Throughout his career, Hogan had many times grumbled about what he called putting's overimportance. But that Saturday at Merion, playing his 36th hole of the day on weary legs and barely recovered from the horrific auto accident that had nearly taken his life 18 months earlier, it wasn't that majestic full swing that won Hogan the national championship. It was his courage and skill with the putter that was the ultimate difference between victory and defeat.

The story of Hogan and Merion is a good place to begin our discussion of putting. No element of the golf game is as crucial to your scoring as the game on the greens, and nowhere is it easier to turn three shots into two (and two into one, for that matter) than on the putting surface. It is the easiest and most rewarding to practice, and it has the greatest potential to let you rapidly improve your scores. So let's get to it.

A Putting Theory

Stating it as simply as I can, all we need to do to become better putters is to hit the ball the correct distance and direction. No kidding. What's so hard about that? But if it were that easy, you probably wouldn't be reading this book and just about everybody in the golf teaching business would be out of work. As simple as it sounds, and as simple as it looks, putting is like watching a duck gliding across the surface of a pond. So natural and smooth and effortless, it seems. But hidden below the surface the duck's feet are working madly to keep him afloat. Even though putting looks straightforward—roll the ball on the right line with the right pace—it is almost infinitely varied and complex. Now, I'm not trying to turn the simple act of rolling the ball on a green into nuclear physics. Heck, I know four-year-old kids and 80-year-old grandmothers who can negotiate themselves around a miniature golf course without that much difficulty. Instead, I'm saying there's more than meets the eye when it comes to this element of your short game. Remember, putting is much more than rolling your ball to the hole, the way they do at the local Putt-Putt. You need to factor in the slope of the green, the condition and type of the grass, the state of the match, and in some cases the strength of the wind. And, of course, you have to have a stroke you can rely on when you're under pressure.

Given all that could be going on "beneath the surface," the key to giving yourself the best chance at making your putts go in the right direction and the right distance is to focus on what you're doing before you start your putting stroke. Get your setup, your aim, your alignment, your ball position, your posture, and your grip organized in such a way that success is more likely than failure.

Then, pay attention to what happens as the putter moves back and forth in your putting stroke. What are your arms and hands doing? What is the face of your putter doing? And, more important, what are you thinking about? Is it the right thing? Should it be something specific? Should you be thinking anything at all?

Finally, work on a solid pre-putt routine that will help you better feel the distance and direction your putt needs to go. Reading greens comes from experience, but knowing what to look for and how to look for it can speed up that learning curve.

■ Jones's Toughest, Biggest Putt

The great Bobby Jones was nearly a cult figure by the late 1920s. Huge throngs followed his every shot in the major championships, and he seemed always favored, almost expected to emerge with another significant championship. In fact, Jones won nine of the 17 majors he played in between 1923 and 1929. (Of course, he would win all four he played in the following year, which gave him the Grand Slam.)

But before 1930 came an especially important moment at Winged Foot Golf Club's West Course in Mamaroneck, New York, in the 1929 U.S. Open. With four holes to play, Jones had a comfortable three-stroke lead on Al Espinosa, who had already finished his final round. But a Jones triple bogey on the 15th hole followed by a three-putt on the 16th left the two players tied. Jones would have to par the difficult final two holes just to force a playoff the next day. On the final green, Jones was left with a testing sidehill twelve-footer for par that he would have to make to secure the tie. The putt broke a foot and a half, but trickled into the cup, sparking a celebratory roar from the crowd of thousands gathered at the final green. Jones crushed Espinosa in the 36-hole playoff the next day by 23 strokes. Herbert Warren Wind, the great chronicler of American golf, wrote later, "If Bobby Jones had failed to sink that putt, there is no knowing how such a collapse might have affected a golfer as hypercritical of himself as Jones. There are many who think that the career of Bobby Jones would have tapered off then and there, that there certainly would have been no Grand Slam had he missed that curling twelve-footer."

You can improve all of these things as you practice. You can set up drills and training tricks that will make your stroke more automatic. You can practice in your living room. You can play putting games with yourself or friends. Above all, get into the habit of watching the ball go in the hole. In the end, seeing success gets you to start believing in success. And putting is at least as much about confidence as it is about technique. And of course getting solid in your technique goes a long way toward improving your confidence.

In the end, putting comes down to this: Understand your setup and make it simple. Understand your stroke and make it better. Understand your read and make it happen. That's how simple putting is. Ben Hogan liked things that way. Simple. I like things that way. You'll like things that way.

Setup

Part I: The Grip

As with the full swing, the fundamentals of your putting stroke start with the way you hold the club. But unlike the grip for a full swing, the putting grip is a grip in the palms of your hands, not the fingers. This helps the hands work together to keep the face of the putter square to the path of your swing and provides the stability and feel that keys a solid, reliable stroke.

Here are the things I focus on with my putting grip:

1 Think of your hands in a "clapping" or "praying" position (right). In a good putting grip, neither hand should dominate. By placing your hands on the club as equals, you've established the triangle formed by your arms and shoulderline. Maintaining the shape of that triangle throughout your stroke is the sign of a putting stroke that is controlled. As a good checkpoint, make sure the distance between your right elbow and left shoulder stays constant throughout the stroke.

2 Your thumbs should be set on top of the putter grip, on the flat part that faces the target line. In addition to ensuring that neither hand overtakes the other in the putting stroke, resting the thumbs on top of the shaft keeps your hands in perfect position to work together as a unit in the stroke (right). With the thumbs on top of the grip, the back of your left hand and the palm of your right hand mirror the face of the putter. Keeping the thumbs on top of the grip but in control also enhances feel and activates the outside shoulder muscles. You want your putting stroke controlled by the big muscles of your shoulders because this is the best way to produce a smooth

stroke. Relying on the fast twitch muscles of your wrists and hands tends to produce inconsistent contact and an unreliable path to the swing of your putter.

3 Position the grip of your putter in the lifeline of your left palm, so your left forearm and the shaft are at the same angle (see photos on page 18). Again, this is a sure way to eliminate excessive—and unreliable—wrist action. With this relationship between grip and shaft, you will be set up to produce the ideal one-lever stroke. In other words, to promote accuracy and consistency in your putting, your arms and the putter should move as one unit, and that's easier to do with the grip of the putter aligned with the lifeline of your left palm.

WARNING: Be careful that you don't force your hands or arms into an unnatural position. Your arms should hang

 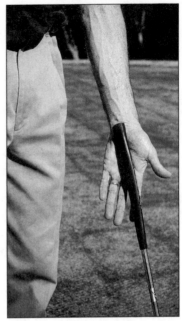

comfortably, not be contorted. And your grip pressure should be gentle, even though your hands are in complete control of the club. You want your grip to be firm enough to be in command of the club, but not so extreme or excessive that you are unable to easily produce a smooth stroke. Squeezing the grip tenses up your muscles, preventing a smooth, flowing stroke. Without a smooth stroke, it will be difficult to get your putts on the proper line.

Part II: Alignment

You can do everything exactly perfectly with your putting stroke, but if you aren't aimed and aligned correctly, none of that really matters. Of course, alignment in golf is not an especially natural motion. If anything, it is especially unnatural. You are not looking at your target (the hole, or the line of your putt), you are looking down at the ball. But there are keys to your aim that can make your setup feel a little more natural.

Here are mine:

1 Because the putting stroke is relatively short, and because there generally isn't a lot of movement and manipulation of the club face during the stroke, setting up the club face correctly toward the target is crucial. It's simple physics: the ball only goes where the club face is aimed. That means you have to aim the club face first, and align your body according to the position of the club face.

2 Though many different setups have worked for putters over the years—Sam Snead even putted by setting up "side-saddle" to the line of the putt and then employed a modified croquet stroke—the most efficient alignment is one where the shoulders and hips remain parallel to the target line (right). From this setup it is easier to make a pendulum stroke, and it is the most efficient, repeatable method for making putts.

3 Maintain the triangle formed by your hands and arms and shoulder line (see photo on page 20). In this tringle, your forearms should be set at an angle parallel to the angle of the shaft. This should be natural, not forced. It may feel more comfortable to have your hands lower and your forearms not in line with the shaft, but trust me—that position leads to inconsistent contact. Remember, you want the putting stroke to be made with the more reliable larger muscles on the outside of your shoulders.

Part III:
Ball Position

Setting up with the ball in the proper position should look natural. But making it look natural and, more important, making it a functional element of a solid putting stroke requires a certain amount of attention to detail. So make it look automatic, but don't take it for granted. Focus on these key points.

1 The ball must be played slightly forward of the breast bone (right). A good rule of thumb is about three inches forward of center, or about the width of two golf balls.

2 Why forward? Since the right hand is lower than the left in a conventional putting grip, the swing arc of the putting stroke bottoms out at a point slightly forward of center.

3 If you choose to play the ball off the left foot, a fairly common guideline, remember this trick: At address lean slightly toward the target with your torso, so that the bottom of your stroke matches the point where the ball is positioned.

Part IV: Posture

How important is your posture? Well, it and it alone determines the type of stroke you will make. How you stand and how your arms hang should match the way you move the putter back and forth. Look at these points:

1 Bend from your hips and slightly from the neck until the eyes are directly over the ball and target line (right). This provides you with a better view of the line. If your eyes aren't directly above the line, you'll be more prone to a misread.

2 Your hands should hang directly underneath and in line with your shoulders. This position lets the arms and

■ Hale's Hellacious Half-Acre Hole-out

Was it 45 feet, 50 feet, or 60 feet? It doesn't really matter. The thing everybody will remember about Hale Irwin's magical putt at the 1990 U.S. Open is that it went in and he went wild. Hale Irwin had won two U.S. Opens before in grinding, gritty fashion, but his third triumph was a highlight reel. He made four birdies on the back nine of the final round, but when he left his approach shot on 18 well short of the hole, it appeared his run might fall one shot short. The putt took about five feet of break, but rolled right into the center of the cup for an almost improbable birdie. The normally stoic Irwin leaped into the air and ran around the green, high-fiving those outside the gallery ropes as he went by. His 280 total would stand as the best of the tournament, tied only by Mike Donald. Irwin won on the 19th hole of the Monday playoff, but he wouldn't have been there without the previous day's miracle. "In 22 years of golf," Irwin said, "I've never made a putt like that to win or come close to winning. It was four times longer than any putt I made all week." But it was Greg Norman, Irwin's playing partner on Sunday, who best summed up the putt. "I guarantee you," he said Sunday night, "that putt won him the U.S. Open."

shoulders move in a more repeatable and consistent path, keeping the face of your putter square to the arc of your putting stroke.

3 There is no one correct posture. Let your style of putting stroke determine your posture. If you stand tall, your arms should hang fairly straight, and your stroke will have a longer, flowing backswing and a shorter follow-through (right). The blade of the putter in this stroke works from open to the target line to closed on the follow-through. (Players to watch: Phil Mickelson, Ben Crenshaw, Bob Charles.)

If you're slightly hunched over with both arms slightly angled and your right arm bent more than your left, you want your stroke to cover the same distance back and

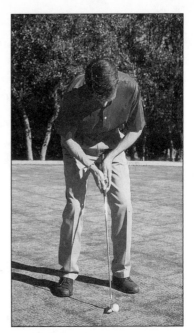

through (above left). Here, the blade works from open to square to the target line. (Players to watch: Tiger Woods, Greg Norman, Mark O'Meara, Brad Faxon.)

If you bend much more from the hips, make sure you keep your arms closer to your body and bend them more from your elbows, too (above right). This is more of a popping stroke with a shorter backswing and a longer follow-through; the blade stays square to the target line throughout the stroke. (Players to watch: Jack Nicklaus, Dave Stockton, Jim Furyk.)

The Stroke

You can have a perfect setup, ideal aim and alignment, an exemplary grip, and super posture, but none of that gets the ball into the hole. Hitting putts or, better, "rolling the ball" correctly is mostly about the stroke. In general, the putting stroke has evolved over the years. Even as recently as 20 years ago, players could get away with a wristy, popping motion at impact. Greens that might have measured a 7 or 8 on the Stimpmeter in the past today are maintained at a speed of 11 or 12. In other words, the greens of 20 and 30 years ago are essentially the fairways of today. At that speed, a pop just won't provide the consistency of contact that superfast greens demand. Today, with greens increasingly faster than they have ever been, a smoother stroke is the most common method for the game's best players. It's also the most successful and the easiest to emulate.

A good way to approach your putting stroke is to think only of moving the grip of the putter back and forth simply by rocking the shoulders up and down (below). Obviously, you want the face of the putter square to your target line at impact, but it shouldn't be manipulated by the hands to get

into this position. Instead, focus your attention on the shaft. At every position in the putting stroke, the shaft should be pointing to a spot on your target line. To be honest, this is where the putter naturally wants to go. There should be no more effort in making this motion than there is in clapping your hands. Trying to keep the face of the putter square throughout the stroke, the so-called "straight back and straight through" method, is an unnatural, forced motion (just see how difficult it is to keep your palms facing each other while moving your hands directly toward an imaginary target). An unnatural stroke is a sure route to inconsistency.

The Key to Consistency

Another way to promote consistency is to match up the length of your backstroke with the length of your follow-through. In other words, the distance the head of your putter travels should be the same on both sides of the ball. This isn't just an abstract point or simply some form of golf teacher-speak; it has a direct impact on your results. If your backstroke and follow-through are different lengths, there's a good chance you're missing putts in a specific way. For example, if you take it back longer and finish shorter, your hands have gotten too active as the putter approaches impact. The result usually is a pull. On the other hand, take it back a little shorter and have a much longer follow-through, and I'll bet you push a lot of putts. The reason? You're probably forcing the face of your putter to stay square to the target line. That's a guaranteed push.

A good way to make sure your stroke is of even measure is to pay attention to that triangle formed by your hands, arms, and shoulders. Make a few practice strokes, pausing to check the shape of that triangle at address, at the end of your backstroke, at impact, and at the end of your follow-through. The shape should be consistent. Just as important, you want to keep the shaft perpendicular to the path of your stroke. The shaft should never be angled ahead of or behind the ball.

Pay attention to angles and feel. First, you'll promote more consistency of contact by maintaining the flex in your elbows throughout the stroke. Change the angle at which your elbows are bent and you can count on one thing: your right hand has overtaken your left and it becomes that much more difficult to consistently strike your putts.

Second, forget about keeping your head still. Instead, stay steady with your right knee and the last vertebra at the top of your spine (where the label of your golf shirt touches the base of your neck). Your right knee flex provides a good foundation so your upper body is supported by your leg muscles, not your back muscles. Your legs are better weight-bearing muscles than your back. Use them and you'll feel more comfortable in your setup, less forced and strained. Comfort breeds confidence, and good putts start with confidence. And it keeps the lower body solid, avoiding the type of swaying that can lead to inconsistent contact. Feeling firm in the top of your neck controls the upper body, allowing the shoulders to rock up and down around a single point.

One Mind, One Body, One Stroke

As has been mentioned, one of the keys to a good stroke is that the hands, arms, and shoulders work as one piece. That is crucial to success in putting, especially on today's faster greens. The quick-twitch muscles of the hands are too unreliable to roll testy six-foot downhillers, so eliminate those small muscles from having a significant part in your putting stroke. Instead, imagine you are unable to change the position of your wrists, hands, elbows, and shoulders once you hold the putter at address.

You can work on this sensation as you practice. First, try hitting putts with the right hand completely overlapping the left. This drill takes the hands out of the stroke and it keeps the left hand leading the putter through the entire stroke. Remember, the right hand should never work faster than the left.

Second, while hitting practice putts, keep the grip pressure constant and hold your finish position. By focusing on the finish, you eliminate any hit in your stroke. Focusing on the hit leads to a less reliable path for the putter head and inconsistent contact. Inconsistent contact makes it impossible to hit putts at the right speed and very difficult to rely on the line you've hit a putt.

A reliable putting stroke is one in which the ball simply gets in the way of the club head. It seems silly to pull an example from the movies, but in *The Legend of Bagger Vance*, Bagger is teaching the young Hardy about feeling his authentic swing. Hardy is told to make a smooth putting stroke back and through, with his eyes closed. As he finds his rhythm, Bagger slyly pushes a ball in the way of his putter, and of course, young Hardy makes the putt. You could give this a try while practicing with a buddy. It might help you get into the habit of letting the ball get in the way of your stroke instead of "hitting" putts.

Confidence

As in almost any part of the game of golf, you can get bound up in all the technical aspects of putting. The first thing you have to do is learn to trust some basic guidelines. And once you've spent some practice time focusing on them, forget about them.

You don't make putts by thinking about where your thumbs should be on the grip, just as you don't make a left turn while driving by thinking about turning the steering wheel 360 degrees counterclockwise. At some point, it becomes intuitive. Now, don't get me wrong. These fundamentals are important, so important that if you don't review them pretty regularly you'll lose them. But good putting is about confidence more than anything else. Nobody ever won anything—not the fifth flight of the member-guest, not the U.S. Open—who did not possess a certain degree of confidence.

We have seen a lot of the game's great putters over the years at the Academy of Golf Dynamics. They all had their idiosyncrasies, but every one of them possessed one thing that a good putter requires: they all believed they were great putters. Even if they were having a bad streak, they never doubted their proficiency on the green. It wasn't a matter of simply believing or hoping that they were suffering a temporary lull; they knew that one bad stretch wouldn't change their overall ability to make putts. They knew that in their hearts and minds as surely as they knew two and two were four.

Now, to that strong sense of belief in your own great putting, I'd add a corollary that the average golfer needs to take to heart: anybody can be a good putter, because good putters are made, not born. Becoming a great putter is a

■ Nicklaus Does It Again

Poll any panel of golf experts and the 1975 Masters routinely is selected as one of the two or three most electrifying tournaments in major championship history. That glorious event saw the game's three premier players all vying for the coveted green jacket all the way to the final stroke on the 18th green. Jack Nicklaus, Tom Weiskopf, and Johnny Miller hit shot after spectacular shot throughout the day. It was like watching a fireworks show, but the biggest blast didn't come at the end of the festivities.

No, it was not on the 18th green, but on the 16th that Jack Nicklaus won a then unprecedented fifth green jacket. Again, it was the short game that decided things. Nicklaus had left his approach short at the par-3 16th green, 38 feet from the hole. But he stroked the putt confidently up the hill, and as the ball found the bottom of the hole, he and his caddie jumped in the air. "I just knew the break, and when it got six feet from the hole, I felt like I had made it," Jack Nicklaus told *Golf Digest* in a retrospective on the tournament 20 years later. "Why did I get so excited? Maybe it's because I didn't make that many putts I needed to make." Weiskopf, reminiscing for the same story, stands amazed to this day. "It was not a putt you make," he said. "But Jack did it to everybody. No one can think of a putt he missed to lose a major championship."

matter of practice, some positive feedback, and a lot of self-confidence.

Even great putters need some reinforcement every now and then. Here are four confidence builders to try:

1 Practice nothing but short, straight putts for 20 minutes. You see this all the time at PGA Tour events. Nothing helps your confidence go up like watching the ball go in the hole a lot.

2 On the other hand, you might want to try practicing putting to a coin or a tee or a paper clip. Forgetting about the hole allows you to feel the natural rhythm of your stroke. Getting away from the instant evaluation of a miss or a make might be just the ticket to developing a consistent, repeatable swing path.

3 Practice stroking the ball while looking at the hole; alternatively, after looking at the hole, putt with your eyes closed. Here, you'll be totally into your target and what it takes to roll the ball to that target. You won't be preoccupied with details. It will just be you-ball-hole, which is all you should be thinking about once you step up to hit a putt on the golf course anyway.

4 Practice at home or in the office. Getting away from the course again takes some of the pressure off your stroke in terms of results. It lets you concentrate on the path of your stroke working on the target line. It also helps develop familiarity. Your putter should be as reliable as your best friend, so spend some time with it even away from the golf course.

Confidence and its application to putting is an individual thing. Pay attention to what works best for you. Maybe focusing on the target is the key to freeing up your stroke. Maybe being a little more nonchalant about results will improve your success by taking some of the pressure off. Decide which approach gives you the greatest comfort level by having little putting contests with yourself or your friends. Are you the type of person who wants all the details before he acts? Then take that attitude with your putting game. Are you more of a freewheeler in business and life? If so, paying attention to every aspect of your putting game before you pull the trigger could leave you feeling bogged down and preoccupied, and lacking the focus you need to be an effective putter. Know yourself, play within yourself, and your confidence level will grow.

The Six Keys

The best putters in the world all have six characteristics.

1 They align the club face to the target, and they align themselves (knees, hips, and shoulders) parallel to their target line.

2 They stay steady with the base of the neck and their legs.

3 They maintain the hands-arms-shoulders triangle so all three work as one.

4 The length of the stroke is the same going back from the ball as it is following through past the ball.

5 They swing the shaft of the putter back and through on the target line without manipulating the blade during the stroke.

6 Confidence. Confidence. Confidence.

Cross-Handed Putting

Jim Furyk, one of the best putters on the PGA Tour, likes to tell the story of how he came to use the cross-handed putting grip. Furyk didn't switch to the unconventional grip after he became a pro, as have several other Tour players in the last 10 years (Vijay Singh, Fred Couples, Tom Kite, Padraig Harrington, Karrie Webb, and Se Ri Pak, among others). No, in fact, Jim Furyk has never putted any other way. His father, Mike, a club pro in Pennsylvania, taught him to putt that way after seeking out the wisdom of two of the greatest players in the history of the game, Arnold Palmer and Gary Player. Palmer and Player were playing a local exhibition when the elder Furyk asked them about various aspects of learning the game. Ironically, both Palmer and Player indicated that if they had it all to do over again, they would have chosen to putt cross-handed instead of using the conventional putting grip. Mr. Furyk took that knowledge and passed it on to his son, and that's just one of the reasons Jim Furyk is one of the best putters—and one of the most accomplished players—in the game today.

Why cross-handed? I don't necessarily think it's for every player, but it's an option worth considering. Keeping the left hand below the right hand on your putting grip has two primary benefits:

1 Since the left hand is below the right, your shoulders are now level. In this position, you're more likely to make better and more consistent contact because the head of the putter stays lower longer before and after impact.

2 A greater advantage with cross-handed putting is the way the position of your left hand effectively prevents excessive wrist action in your stroke. With the left hand and arm essentially leading or pulling the putter through the forward stroke, you'll be able to make a smoother move toward the ball. This method makes it very easy to keep the putter square to the target line.

You don't have to make any wholesale changes to your putting stroke in order to switch to cross-handed. (In fact, it may help simplify your stroke by limiting the role of your hands.) Create your stroke by using the larger muscles on the outside of your arms and then rocking your shoulders.

One thing worth checking, though, is your ball position and alignment. Make sure that your putter, shoulders, and hips remain parallel to the target line.

Even though switching to cross-handed is relatively easy, if you're going to switch, make a commitment to your new grip. Spend some time on the putting green working on feel. A cross-handed stroke is very effective on short straight putts, but it requires a great deal of practice on lag putts so that you're able to feel the longer distance putts with your new grip.

Lag Putting

Here are some tips for getting more familiar with the feel of lag putting—in fact, these tips are valid for a conventional stroke, too:

1 If you're going to be a successful putter, you have to be confident with your long-distance putting just as you should be with the short putts. At the Academy of Golf Dynamics, we don't like to think of lagging the long putts. Instead, you should always have the feeling and the final image in your mind as you step over any putt—even the longest putts— that the ball is going into the hole. Remember, a missed lag is almost always a difficult second putt, but a putt that misses going in often can still lead to a fairly easy second putt.

2 Focus on the last two feet of any longer putt. Ideally, that's where your ball will be slowing down, and as a putt slows down, it's going to be that much more affected by the undulations on the green. After you read the putt and set your putter on your intended line, forget about the first part of your putt or what the ground feels like where you're standing. The last two feet of the putt should be the only thing on your mind.

3 Hit practice putts from various distances, but don't look up from your putts to follow the ball. Instead, guess (long left, short right, etc.). When you start guessing correctly without looking, you know your stoke is starting to match your visualization. In short, you're developing the kind of feel that breeds consistently successful putting.

4 Instructors and others often talk about the three-foot-radius circle they're trying to get their longer putts to stop in. I say forget that. Instead, think about making even the long putts. Get in the habit of visualizing the ball going into the hole and the type of stroke that's going to be required to get the ball to roll the correct distance. Think of it this way: If you're aiming for the hole and miss by three feet (not unusual for a longer putt), you have a three-footer left. But if your target is a three-foot circle and you miss the perimeter by three feet, you're left with a six-footer.

Reading Greens

When Payne Stewart won the 1999 U.S. Open with a par-saving 15-foot putt on the 18th hole, it was a great stroke, a great moment—but most of it all it was a great read. Reading greens starts with experience. And it ends in trust and self-reliance. That's exactly what Stewart experienced on that 18th green with the U.S. Open hanging in the balance. After his round, he told reporters, "I knew it was going to go to the right. Even though the mound there wanted to influence it the other way, I just knew in my mind that it was going to go to the right a little. I just said to myself, this is an inside-left putt, just believe that. And I stood up there and did my routine and kept my head still and when I looked up it was about two feet from the hole and it was breaking right in the center and I couldn't believe it."

Stewart had practiced that putt earlier in the week. He had practiced putting a great deal all week long, as a matter of fact. The importance of that experience and that comfort level with the conditions cannot be understated. There is no replacement for hitting lots of putts on the putting green and getting a good sense of how the ball will react on the greens you're going to putt today. In fact, if you only have a few minutes to get ready for your round, I'd advise spending a little time stretching and then spending the rest of the time on the putting green.

In addition to putting in practice time and developing a feel for distance and direction, there are six guidelines I use to help me in reading greens. Of course, it's important to remember that these are general ideas on how putts will break. They shouldn't be a substitute for lining up your putts individually with your pre-putt routine.

1 Pay attention to the lay of the land around the green. Generally, the topography of the land in the vicinity of the green will affect the way putts will break on the green. For example, if the green is set at the base of a slope, it's fair to assume that most putts will break away from that slope. If there are no context clues in the immediate area, check in the distance. If you have doubts, check any topographical features within your view. A hill to your right is a sure sign that, all other things being equal, putts will break to your left. And remember, putts break more the slower they're rolling.

■ The Short Man's Longest Putts

"Gentlemen, the next three holes you will not believe." Those were the words Jerry Barber used to describe to golf writers his final-round finish at the 1961 PGA Championship. Trailing his playing partner, Don January, by four strokes, Barber played the final three holes in two under, and January made two bogeys, to leave the players tied. Barber would win the playoff the next day, becoming at 45 the oldest ever to win the PGA title. He was also the smallest, at five feet five inches and 137 pounds. Barber's birdie-par-birdie comeback is an amazing enough feat on its own, until you consider just how Barber played his final three holes in regulation. At the 16th hole, Barber made a 20-footer for birdie. Then, on 17, struggling to reach the green in three shots, he rammed home a 40-footer for par. Finally, on 18, still trailing by two shots, Barber rolled home an outlandish 60-footer for birdie. The last putt had some four feet of break but rolled smoothly in the hole as if it had been struck from one tenth that distance. Barber once remarked that the short game was the key to his success. "I was good enough at one point in my career that when I missed a green, it really didn't bother me," he said. "I realized I could become as good at the short game as anyone, or even better, so I worked at it very hard."

2 When you approach the green, take a look at the angle the flagstick is entering the ground on the green. It should be relatively easy to see whether one area around the hole appears higher than another. Putts break from that higher side toward the lower side.

3 Generally speaking, putts break away from mountains and toward water. Even if the green isn't surrounded by a pond, there may be a pond elsewhere on the course, and generally, your putts will break toward the closest body of water. Check with a local or the starter or the club pro to see if there's a general rule of thumb as to the direction putts break. For instance, the Baltusrol Golf Club in Springfield, New Jersey, a famous U.S. Open site, is set at the foot of Baltusrol Mountain. The obvious general rule of thumb is to look for the mountain when you're on the green and note that your putts will break away from that mountain.

4 It's certainly worth paying attention to the grain of the grass on the putting green—the direction the blades point—though its impact on putts is less than many TV announcers suggest it to be. This is particularly true on Bermuda grass greens. Here are some tricks for reading grain. The grain of the grass is the direction in which it grows. Grass grows toward the setting sun, and from this angle the grass blades appear shiny. Putts in this situation are said to be "downgrain." Conversely, when the grass looks dull from a particular angle, it means putts will be rolling in the opposite direction that the grass blades are leaning. Putts in this situation are said to be "into the grain." Downgrain putts will be faster than normal; into-the-grain putts will be slower.

5 Pay attention to what your feet are telling you. Slope naturally affects your balance, so if you sense yourself drifting to one side or the other as you walk onto the green, file this away. Also, if there is slope in your putt left or right, you should be able to feel a little more weight on one foot than the other. Again, this is evidence you can use for predicting whether your putt will break to one side or the other.

6 Watch everyone else putt. It's against the rules of golf to stand on another player's line as he's hitting the ball, but it's certainly well within your rights to quickly slide over and take a look once he's hit the putt. Remember, though, how a putt breaks is largely a function of speed. If someone hits the ball with more speed than you do, his putt will break less. But again, it should give you a general idea, and you should use every little piece of information to make sense of your putt.

Reading greens is part science, part art, and part intuition and faith. But it begins and ends with practice and experience. The more you understand how the ball comes off the face of your putter and how the ball will move naturally on the green, the more confidence you will have when it comes your turn to putt. If you want to learn to understand break, devote a putting practice session or two to hitting a variety of breaking putts. Don't focus on getting the ball into the hole. Pay attention instead to how the ball is curving, where it slows down, and when it picks up speed. Understand these first, and getting the ball to go in the hole will take care of itself.

Short-Putt Secrets

Nothing seems so easy yet can cause so much stress and grief and anxiety and make us look so inept as the short putt. There are no easy answers that will make the trials and tribulations of short putts disappear, but here are some tips that will allow you to make those testy short putts seem a little easier.

1 Have a simple but repeatable pre-putt routine and follow it explicitly with every putt of any significance. Getting involved in that process will occupy your mind and allow your body to make the stroke. Do the same thing for every putt: think only of that routine and you won't have room to worry about negative results.

2 Watch your grip. Maintaining consistent, even grip pressure should take the hit out of your stroke. If there's any hit in your stroke, you've allowed your right hand to get too active, and that makes it less likely that your putt will stay on the proper line.

3 Don't focus on the club face; focus on the handle. Feel the handle work back and forward. The face of your putter is an extension of the handle. It's also easier to control because it moves a shorter distance. But remember, consciously accelerating the putter can leave the face of the putter open, leading to poor direction and inconsistent distance control.

4 Keep your head down. Listen for the ball to go into the hole. If you keep your head down, you'll be pleasantly surprised at what you might hear.

5 Play with your stance. If you feel as though your head is moving too much on your follow-through, try a closed stance. It makes looking up more of an effort. However, if you tend to look down to the point where you're not paying enough attention to the target, try opening up your stance. Seeing the hole may remind you what the ultimate object of your stroke should be.

The Power of the Left Hand

If either hand takes control of your putting stroke, it should be your left hand. Think of the left hand pulling the putter handle through the hitting zone on the forward stroke. The pulling motion of the left hand is more reliable than a pushing motion by the right hand. You can pull something with a hinge straighter than you can push it. Imagine pushing a wagon loaded down with bricks. Is it going to roll straighter if you push it from behind or pull it with the handle? Things with a hinge (a wagon, your putting stroke) move straighter when they are pulled, not pushed. When you pull it, you keep all your joints (wrist, elbow, and shoulder) working together in the same direction. When you push, the wrists, elbows, and shoulders can work against each other instead of together.

Pre-putt Routine

There is no substitute for proper technique, but consistent, reliable putting starts with a solid, repeatable routine before every putt. What you do to line up a putt is strictly up to you, but if you get in the habit of doing the same thing before every putt, it will make you more comfortable with every putt, regardless of the circumstances. The following is a good routine to follow. With this or any other routine, make your routine something easy for you to do; keep it simple and efficient. The purpose of a pre-putt routine is to get a sense of the line and the speed of the putt, rehearse the stroke, and finally put you in the frame of mind to make a smooth, confident stroke. Try this method.

1 As you approach the ball, get an initial read of the line and speed by noting any general slope to the green.

2 Mark the ball and gauge the line from behind the ball.

3 Set the line in your mind as you take your stance over the ball, looking at the hole.

4 Make a practice stroke that is an exact match of the actual stroke you'll need to make. Again, looking at the hole while you make the practice stroke helps ingrain your sense of distance.

5 As you turn your head back to look down at the ball, get settled first, pause, and then make the stroke.

Equipment Tips

Finding the Right Putter for You

Jesper Parnevik likes to say he uses so many different putters because he goes with what feels good on a particular day or in a particular week. There's no rhyme nor reason to it, except he knows what's going to give him confidence and he goes with that. Of course, if you look at the putters he uses, they are generally pretty similar. So there is method to his madness. You should have a method for selecting your putter, too, and you just might end up making more putts.

Before we begin talking about the keys to selecting the right putter, there are some ground rules. There are four basic design styles of putters:

- The heel-toe weighted putter. (Example: The Ping Anser-like offset models, Scotty Cameron)

- The blade design. (Example: The classic Wilson 8802 Model)

- Mallet or thick blade designs. (Example: Ray Cook M-1X, Ram Zebra, Odyssey Rossie II)

- Center-shafted models. (Example: Bulls Eye, Never Compromise Zi-alpha)

There are two elements that determine what putters particular players use.

- Cosmetics—look and feel

- Length and speed of stroke

Here are the types of putters most often used and the types of players who choose them.

Heel-toe weighted, slightly offset

This is the most popular model of putter used by professional golfers worldwide. Use this putter if your stroke is an arm and shoulder motion where the putter shaft goes straight back and straight through with a consistent, not overly quick or slow motion. Generally, the length of the backstroke matches the length of the follow-through. Players like Greg Norman, Tiger Woods, David Duval, Loren Roberts, and Brad Faxon use this type of putter.

Blade Putters

If the stroke is long and flowing, where the face of the putter opens on the backswing and closes on the forward swing, then a blade putter is for you. Players: Ben Crenshaw, Phil Mickelson, Lee Trevino, and Larry Mize.

Mallet Putters

Players with firm, compact strokes where the right hand creates the power and the left hand stays on for control will benefit more from a mallet putter. Players: Dave Stockton, Nick Price, Nancy Lopez, Billy Casper.

Center-shafted Putters

These putters work best for players who make an arm stroke. Generally, if you keep the putter especially low to the ground on the backswing, the center-shafted putter works best. Players: Tom Kite, Bob Charles, Payne Stewart.

■ Stockton's "Usual" Wins PGA

The legendary golf writer Dan Jenkins once wrote of the two-time PGA champion Dave Stockton, "He is the kind of player of whom his contemporaries say, 'Dave shot an eighty but turned in his usual sixty-nine.'" In other words, Stockton's short game and putter could make up for a lot of mistakes elsewhere on the course. His second PGA Championship, in 1976 at suburban Washington, D.C.'s, Congressional Country Club, was a perfect example. Stockton shot a final-round 70 to win by a single shot, but he did so while only hitting nine greens in regulation, including just three in his final nine holes. Like a champion, he saved his best tricks for last. At the 17th hole, with his ball tucked under the lip of a bunker and a long way from the hole, he neatly blasted out to three feet and confidently rolled home the putt. But at 18 it would get even tougher. Leading by a single stroke, Stockton left his second short of the peninsula green, then chipped onto the green 12 feet short of the hole. But after studying his putt from every angle, Stockton rolled the par-saving putt right into the heart of the hole. "It was uphill, inside the right corner," Stockton said. "Easy." Just what you'd expect a man with a rock-solid short game to say.

Choosing a Putter

Now, how do you go about choosing the right putter? I think there are four basic criteria for selecting the putter that will let you putt your best.

Style

Decide which of the putter styles best fits your typical putting stroke. The look of the putter shouldn't be a distraction. It should promote comfort and confidence. Pay particular attention to how you line up a putter. It should be easy for you to align the putter to your target. If you're not sure, try a little test. Go to the putting green with several different putters and a friend. Have your friend stand behind you as you line up several 5- to-7-foot putts. Have your friend note how often you naturally line up each putter correctly. If one naturally lines up more easily for you, then that's the style you want to focus your search on.

Length

The length of the putter that works best for you is a direct result of your posture at address. The taller you stand naturally, the longer a putter you should use. Remember, when you bend the hips at address and grip the putter, your eyes should be directly over the ball. Also, a longer putter will be significantly heavier, and of course, a heavier putter can alter the tempo of your swing. But a longer putter also would be a good fit to promote a long smooth stroke. That's why it's such a good fix for the yips.

Lie

A poor lie angle makes it doubly difficult to get your putts started on the right line. Too upright, and a good stroke still could lead to putts that roll right of the target; too flat, and you may miss it left. Obviously, you want a putter that feels comfortable with your posture while you keep the putter lying flat on the ground. A good way to determine the correct lie is to take your address position on a flat floor with your hands in a comfortable spot resting directly below your shoulders, while you bend at the waist with your eyes directly over the ball. If the heel and toe of the putter both are on the ground without any manipulation of the hands, then the putter has the right lie angle for you. If the toe is up, then you need a putter with a more upright lie angle; if the heel is up, you need a little flatter lie.

Weight

A putter of a different weight may be better suited to your style of putting or even the conditions you normally play. Here are three things to pay attention to:

1 Generally speaking, heavier putters are better on slower greens; light putters are more effective on fast greens. A heavier putter will let you impart a little more force to your putts without having to alter your stroke. In the same way, a lighter putter lets you make a more flowing stroke (in other words, less of a jabbing motion) without fear that the ball will take off on a superfast green.

2　A heavier putter works better if your stroke is naturally longer and slower; a lighter putter is best for strokes that are shorter and quicker.

3　If you tend to grip your putter tightly, a heavier putter might provide you with a better feel.

Putting Myths

We've spent some time talking about what's worth doing with your putting stroke. Now, it's time to talk about some things not worth paying attention to. Let's call these putting myths.

■ **"The blade stays square to the target line throughout the stroke."**

Believing and acting on this idea leads to a forced motion with the hands to manipulate the face of the putter during the swing. But the best putting strokes are a natural smooth motion. In a natural stroke, the face is truly square only at address and ideally at impact. Remember, because the putter shaft is at an angle to the club head and because you stand to the side of the the club to swing it, the face of the putter will naturally fan open slightly on the backswing and then close slightly on the forward swing.

■ **"Good putters consciously accelerate on the forward swing to the ball."**

We've all heard the expression "Don't quit on it" to describe a putting stroke where we decelerated on the forward stroke and didn't keep the putter moving at a consistent pace up to impact and into the follow-through. But there is a difference between "accelerating" and "not decelerating." Any attempt to accelerate on the forward stroke naturally will cause the handle to move faster than the club head, which means the shaft will lean too far forward and the face will be open to the target line at impact. Instead, concentrate on keeping the length of the backstroke the same as the length of the follow-through. Consistent pace should produce consistent success.

■ **"The feet need to line up to the target."**

Except in unusual situations, the feet should at most be parallel to the target line. But only two things determine aim and alignment and neither are your feet. The ball deflects wherever the putter is aimed at impact, and the arms swing the putter on the line of the shoulders. Keep your shoulders parallel to the target line to make a consistent stroke down the target line.

■ **"Good putters keep the putter low."**

Think of the putting stroke as a mini–full swing. Just as the club head of an iron or wood naturally gets well above the ground, so should the small swing of the putter travel slightly up on the backstroke, then slightly down on the forward swing and then slightly up again on the follow-through.

Forcing it low means you will have to change the bend in your elbows during the stroke, and that's a sure way to lead to inconsistent contact.

■ "Good putters try to roll the ball over an intermediate spot between the ball and the hole."

This is a tricky one, but because putting is about distance as much as direction, you need to make your aiming point about even with the distance of the hole. This will help you roll your putts the proper distance as well as direction.

That said, there is an exception to this rule. I learned the value of this measuring trick by watching the old caddies at St. Andrews in Scotland. At the Old Course, you can have a lot of putts that are significantly uphill or downhill. To help their players gauge speed, wise old caddies would often take the flagstick out of the hole and hover it over the line (touching the ground with the pin is violation of the rules of golf). The old caddies would hold the stick short of the hole for downhill putts, but well past the hole for uphill putts. If you have a downhill putt, make your target a little short of the hole. If the putt is uphill, make your target slightly past the hole. This imagery will help you roll the ball at the right pace to give it a chance to go in.

■ "Uphill putts should be hit harder; downhill putts should be hit easier."

Hitting an uphill putt hard can lead to a pushed putt because the handle of the putter races ahead of the club face, leaving it open at impact. Hitting a downhill putt softly causes the hands to slow down, allowing the club face to outrace the handle, closing the face and making putts roll left of the target. Instead of thinking "harder/easier," think distance. To help instill the notion of how pace will change depending on the slope of the green, on uphill putts, pick a target past the hole. On downhill putts pick a target that is short of the hole.

Putting Drills

Toe putts

To build the idea that you're swinging the shaft of the putter, not the club head, rotate the club 90 degrees so that the toe of the putter is pointing down the target line. Then, hit putts with the toe of the putter, making solid contact and rolling the ball on a straight line.

Path fix

If your putting stroke is an outside-to-in motion, making consistent sweet-spot hits on the face of the putter a random occurrence, use two clubs set on either side of the ball to groove the proper stroke. Place one club just behind, parallel to, and to the outside of the target line (above). Then, place the second club just in front of, parallel to, and inside the target line. These club "guardrails" should keep the club from drifting too far outside the target line on the backswing and too far inside on the follow-through. If your problem is more an inside-to-out swing, then simply reverse the position of the guide clubs.

Shoulder fix

If your swing tends to be controlled too much by the rocking of your shoulders but is lacking feel, set up with your feet together or your legs criss-crossed. This setup gets the arms swinging more from the shoulder sockets.

Handy fix

If your hands dominate your stroke, you can get the shoulders back into the stroke by holding the shaft of the putter parallel to the ground and in your fingers (below). Simply rock the shaft back and forth from this position to develop the appropriate shoulder motion.

■ Price's Turnberry Heroics

In 1994, Nick Price was among the best ball strikers the game of golf had ever seen, but it was a cagey short game and an inspired putt that gave him the major championship he coveted the most. At the 1994 British Open, Price came to the final nine holes trying to chase down the then young upstart Jesper Parnevik. Missing some chances on the front nine, Price righted himself with crucial miraculous chip shots on the 13th and 14th holes. On 14, in fact, Price ran a seven-iron chip along the ground while marshals and fans held a television cable high in the air. The shot nearly went in. But the deciding shots came at the end. After a brilliant approach to the par-5 17th, Price faced a 50-foot putt for eagle and thought about making it. "I knew I had to make that putt," he said. "I *had* to make that putt. But I couldn't believe it went in. I just about jumped out of my skin." After the shocker at 17, Price had the lead and still needed to negotiate 30 feet in two putts for the win. He did so patiently, going through the same careful routine he'd used all week.

"It's amazing," he said. "I reached down deep inside and surprised myself. I knew I had it in me, but things like that don't usually happen when you need it most. Today it did. It's like a fairy-tale ending."

Underarm solution

To get the hands, arms, and shoulders to work together and maintain the triangle formed by your upper body, slide a club between your elbows and torso and practice your stroke (right). If all the parts are working together, the club under your arms should stay there throughout the stroke.

Double overlap fix

At the Academy of Golf Dynamics, we often see players struggle with their putting because they tend to take the putter back more with the left hand and then bring it back through with the right hand dominating. This leads to the wrists breaking down before impact, which results in inconsistent, off-line contact. To fix it, practice putting by using a putting grip where the right hand completely overlaps the left hand (below). This takes the hands out of the stroke and gets you focused on generating power in the putting stroke from the rocking of the shoulders and swinging of the arms, not the hinging of the wrists.

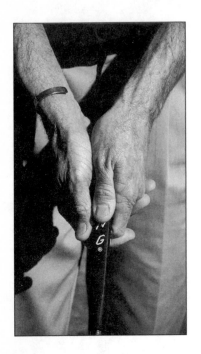

Blocking fix

If you feel as though you're forcing the club face to stay square on the forward swing well into your follow-through, you may be pushing putts right of the target. To combat that feeling, hit some practice putts with a split grip with the index finger of your right hand pointing down the shaft (see photo on page 57). This grip will encourage the club to move in a natural motion with the face opening slightly on the backswing and closing on the follow-through. Another check to avoid this problem is to try to keep the left elbow close to the body on the follow-through.

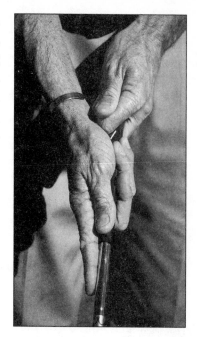

Distance fix

If you're having trouble developing a sense of distance, try hitting putts with your eyes closed and see how consistently you can roll putts the same distance. Another drill is to keep your head down and guess how far each putt rolled.

Scoring drill

To get control of your lag putting, hit six sets of three putts from 20 to 40 feet and to a different collection of six holes. That makes for a total of "18 holes." For scoring purposes, a ball finishing within the length of a putter is a par, in the hole is a birdie and outside the length of a putter is a bogey. Your goal is to score even par.

Balancing act

To keep yourself steady on shorter putts, hit some practice putts with your sand wedge leaning against your right thigh (see photo on page 58). This will fix two flaws. First, it will keep the putter going straight back and straight through (if

you take it back too far outside, you'll bump into the
shaft of the sand wedge).
Second, it will keep the lower
body steady (sway a little bit
with your legs and the sand
wedge will fall to the ground).

Wedge control

To groove a one-lever pendulum stroke, try hitting 20
or more putts with your sand
wedge. If there's too much
extra movement in your putting stroke, you'll mis-hit every
putt. This drill also helps
breed good tempo and con-
sistent grip pressure.

CHAPTER TWO

CHIPPING

▼ ▼ ▼ ▼

The Short-Game Shot of a Lifetime

In one sense, Larry Mize was not supposed to win the 1987 Masters. In another, he was perhaps destined for it. Born and raised in Augusta, Georgia, as a teenager Mize had actually worked on one of the scoreboards on the grounds during the annual tournament. In his imagination, he saw himself playing the Augusta National, competing in the Masters, and maybe, just maybe, winning one. But he also knew that was pure fantasy.

Years later, when presented with an opportunity to do the impossible, even Mize knew that thinking he had a chance to win at Augusta National was more than a little bit optimistic. Mize was not a long hitter off the tee, and was a competent though not spectacular iron player, but he could be more than a little special when the ball got around the green. He had exceptional, beautifully rhythmic tempo with every club in his bag, but he was at his silkiest with the short shots. Never one to be overly inventive, Mize knew that the simpler short shot was often the best play. He knew to putt it whenever you could, to chip it if you couldn't putt it, and to pitch it if you couldn't putt it or chip it. Those rules should be yours, too.

At the '87 Masters, when Mize made a gutty birdie on the 72nd hole to get into a playoff, it seemed only a little less unbelievable that he might fulfill his boyhood dream of winning his hometown major. After all, joining him in that playoff were Seve Ballesteros and Greg Norman, without question the two best players in the world at the time. But when Ballesteros fell out on the first hole, the dream started to take shape. Then, Mize misplayed his approach shot on the 11th hole, leaving himself nearly 50 yards from the hole. It would have been easy to get discouraged at that point, to be content with a good showing against the top players in the world, take his second-place money, and move on to the next event. But Mize would not let go of his opportunity just yet. He knew something you should know, too. He knew that a good short game can make up for a lot of errors, even on the grandest stage in golf.

Mize quickly evaluated his situation. A full-blooded pitch might be too firm a shot for the rock-hard Augusta National greens. But he also knew that a good chip (which was also easier) and a straightforward putt could keep him in the playoff, could put the pressure on Norman. Playing the ball back in his stance and using his sand wedge, Mize played a delicate bump-and-run chip, landing the ball short of the ultrafirm green and getting the ball rolling like a putt. The 140-foot chip shot took the left-to-right break and dove into the hole in an instant, shocking Mize even more than the vanquished Norman.

Said Mize at the time, "When you are a little kid, you always have that one big dream you hope will come true.

My dream when I was a little child growing up here finally came true."

Mize hit a very nearly perfect shot in the most pressure-packed circumstances. How did he do it? He took the easiest play, he tried to get the ball close by playing it along the ground, and he executed a shot he had practiced hundreds of times. It took no amount of superhuman strength or speed. In fact, it was something any player might be able to do, even if the only thing at stake is a Coke in the grill room. Good chipping breeds confidence in every element of your game and it keeps you in play on every hole, even if your approach shot misses the pin by nearly 50 yards. Take the short shots to heart, and you'll be surprised at how much your scores improve with the least amount of difficulty.

A Chipping Theory

The chip shot might very well be the easiest off-the-green short-game shot. For average recreational players, it is also probably the most misapplied short-game shot in the book. Why misapplied? Well, I think the average player misunderstands what a chip is supposed to do. The idea behind a chip shot—and why it is such an easy shot to use if executed properly—is to get the ball on the green and rolling as soon as possible. The tried and true phrase in chipping is "minimal air time, maximum ground time." As the great Jack Nicklaus said after learning all the secrets from his short-game mentor, Phil Rogers, "Roll is easier to judge than flight." This is so true. How comfortable are you flying the ball 45 feet? Do you know what length swing will fly the ball that distance every time? No? But I'll bet if you faced a 45-foot putt you could almost immediately know about what type of stroke would get the ball rolling the right distance. That's why you

■ The Overlooked Shot of the Tournament

As is often the case, the big shots that win a major championship can get lost in the excitement at the finish. The crucial shot often is one that occurs in the middle of that final round, not the end. Ernie Els had such a shot that keyed his second U.S. Open victory in 1997. Playing the brutishly long par-4 10th at Congressional Country Club, Els hit his approach shot a little fat and left himself just short of the green. It was a fortunate error because it took the greenside rough and water out of play. Still, he was left with a 30-foot chip, not a guaranteed up-and-down by any means. But certainly it would be a lot easier to make a 3 or a 4 from this position than from the pond by the green. Els deftly ran his lofted chip just onto the green, and the ball rolled directly to the stick, hit it, and went into the hole. While his rivals faltered, Els played solidly the rest of the way to win by one shot. "The tenth was a big swing, you know," Els later said. "I just tried to get it on the front side of the green and take four." Sometimes discretion—and a good short game—is the better part of valor.

should think of your chipping game as an extension of your putting game, not as a cut-down version of your full swing. At the Academy of Golf Dynamics, we do not claim this idea of chipping as our own. It's been around for decades, thanks in large part to the tremendous success of the legendary Paul Runyan. Runyan was a short-game wizard and two-time PGA champion of the 1930s. He did it despite being out-driven by nearly every one of his peers on nearly every hole. He used his guile and his ability to chip, pitch, and putt better than anybody else to frustrate his bigger, bolder opponents. Runyan believed in simplifying the chipping stroke as much as possible, and he explained his thinking in his great instruction textbook, *The Short Way to Lower Scores.*

As Runyan indicated, because chipping is all about precision, you want as few moving parts in your upper and lower body as possible, just as in your putting stroke. You don't have to generate power with chip shots. Instead, let the club you choose (not the swing you make) dictate the power of your shot. If you feel you're pressing to get your chip shot to roll the right distance, just switch to a less lofted club and go back to making a controlled chipping motion.

I think it is important to understand what a chip is because that helps us execute it more successfully. A chip shot should only carry about six paces in the air. If you try to fly it any longer, your chipping technique will be prone to breaking down. Truth be told, flying the ball longer than six steps in the air most likely means you'll need to be hitting a pitch shot. Carrying the ball six paces (or less) is designed to take advantage of the simplest way to get the ball to the hole: rolling it there. Also, a short amount of carry allows us to use a chipping stroke without any wrist action. What we're interested in is a single-lever motion designed to get the ball slightly airborne and then get it rolling on the ground as soon as possible.

Here are my three golden rules for chipping:

1 Use a variety of clubs.

2 Make your target the front of the green. Fly the ball to this point (no farther) and let the ball roll the rest of the way.

3 Hit the ball as firmly as you would a putt of the same length.

Chipping Setup

At the Academy of Golf Dynamics, we believe chipping is a unique aspect of the game, but we also feel that it should be simple to understand and easy to execute. That's why we want chips to be as much like putts as possible. Everybody can putt, and if everybody can putt, then just about everybody should be able to chip. And if you can chip, you're going to have more chances to make a good score than any guy who only knows how to hit the big drive. With the idea in mind that your chipping stroke should be similar to your putting stroke, you should focus on these setup points.

Grip

You can put your hands on the grip in whatever fashion that feels most comfortable to you, but generally we recommend a reverse overlap putting grip, where the index finger of the left hand overlaps the pinky on your right hand. This allows the hands to simply swing the club back and through without any sudden acceleration or inconsistency in your approach to short shots. Keep the club in the middle of your palms. Ideally, you want your hands neutral on the grip, so that neither hand is in a stronger position on the club. Also, square the club face to the target line while keeping the club aligned more at the vertical than at a diagonal. The club shaft should be oriented extremely upright so the toe of the club touches the ground but heel does not. This will help you avoid hitting the ground behind the ball.

Stance

When you're hitting a chip shot you want very little extra body movement and you don't need any significant upper-body rotation to generate power (which would require a wide stable stance). Therefore, you want a fairly simple narrow stance that is slightly open but close to the ball. The open stance will allow the club to work freely back and through, staying in front of your body throughout the stroke. There should be just enough bend at your hips for your eyes to be directly over the target line.

Ball position

Align the ball just off the big toe on your left foot. In addition, the club is positioned so the ball is being played off the toe of the club. Feel as though the center of your chest is shifted slightly toward the target, with your weight concentrated on your left foot. You can even feel as though you're leaning your chest forward of the ball. This will enable you to make a slightly downward stroke on the forward swing of your chip shot. It will impart the right amount of spin while lofting the ball in the air just enough to land it on the green.

FLAW: A common mistake with chip shots is to play the ball too far back in your stance. The feeling is that in order to keep the ball low, you have to play it back. That's true, but it can be overdone. If the ball is too far back, your hands have to make too much of an inside-to-out move to contact the ball. Your hands will get too active trying to get the club face square at impact, while conversely your weight will tend to stay on your back foot. That leads to thinly hit chips that end up running well past your target.

A Chip Trick

I believe the most efficient chipping stroke is one that approximates your putting motion. But to do that, you have to get your shoulders level to the ground at the setup. A good way to find the proper setup position is to maintain a slight bend at your left elbow and your left knee. With your shoulders level, you'll be more able to make a pendulum stroke. However, if your left arm stays straight, your left shoulder is going to be higher than your right and your weight is naturally going to favor your back foot (see left photo). That makes it hard to make the downward stroke on your forward swing. With the weight hanging back, you're more likely to hit a thin shot than one that rolls the proper distance. By keeping the shoulders level, you should feel as though you're making a natural downward move on the forward swing, not a forced chop at the ball, which is inconsistent and involves too much wrist action.

The Chipping Stroke

To hit a chip shot properly, here is what you do not do. You don't scoop. You don't hack. You don't gouge. You shouldn't accelerate on the forward swing, and you shouldn't feel as though you're excessively abbreviating your follow-through.

Instead, focus on making a stroke that is of consistent pace and a consistent length. In short, chipping is about making one simple stroke and changing clubs to fit that same stroke. Here are my guidelines:

Target

All things being equal, you want to land the ball about three feet onto the front of the green. Why? Because the object is to get the ball rolling as quickly as possible. Get your chip shots to behave like putts and you'll have a better gauge of how to get your shots close to the hole (see photos on page 70). Set up a target on the green to get you in the habit of visualizing the proper target.

Swing

The object is to move the whole club back and forth, not just the club head or the grip. The club should move back and forth as if it were on a pendulum suspended from your

■ Janzen Plays Out His Option

Lee Janzen had played in three previous U.S. Opens prior to the 1993 tournament at Baltusrol Golf Club. He had missed the cut each time. So it was a bit of a surprise when he found himself in the final pairing on Sunday afternoon, with Payne Stewart. It was even more of a surprise to see him one stroke ahead of the more experienced Stewart late in the day, especially after Janzen had managed to miss fairways and greens at every other turn. In fact, Janzen hit just six fairways and only 11 greens. But his salvation was the short game. And it provided the crucial stroke in his first major championship victory. Janzen's five-iron to the par-3 16th hole was pulled left of the green, and the ball rested on a mound in the rough about 10 yards from the hole. Despite being farther away from the hole, Stewart, who was on the putting surface, gave Janzen the option to hit first. Seeing the shot he faced as a real scoring opportunity, Janzen calmly took his sand wedge and nudged the ball out of the high grass and onto the green where it rolled into the hole.

The birdie gave Janzen a two-shot advantage that he maintained to win his first U.S. Open title.

"I just felt somehow I was destined," Janzen said later. "I was lucky to have a great lie, and then I hit a great shot.

"I knew if I chipped it in, it's going to be a huge advantage. I asked Payne twice, and he gave me the option to go. I felt like any advantage I could get, I should take."

sternum. Keeping that motion consistent helps you utilize the true distance of the club. You shouldn't feel like you have to help the ball in the air or accelerate the club on the forward swing. Simply swing the club back and forth, letting the ball get in the way and letting the loft of the club get the ball onto the green and rolling like a putt.

FLAW: Avoid any significant wrist hinge on the backswing or the forward swing. If your wrists hinge on the backswing, the club face will shut down, turning an eight-iron to a six-iron and making it that much more difficult to properly judge distance. If your wrists hinge coming through, you'll tend to scoop shots at impact, adding loft and turning your eight-iron into a pitching wedge. That means your shots won't roll as much as you would expect, and you'll end up excessively short of your intended target.

FIXES: If you're battling excessive wrist hinge on the backswing, try the split-grip drill where you hit chips with your hands separated by a few inches on the grip.

If the problem is scooping, or trying to help your shots into the air, use the same trick you might use in your putting stroke. Chip cross-handed. With the left hand below the right hand, you'll keep those wrists from breaking down too early.

Pace

Because your chipping stroke should be an approximation of your putting stroke, a good way to gauge the proper pace of your swing is to imagine you are hitting a putt (on the green) the same distance as your chip. Swing your club, whether it be an eight-iron or a six-iron, with that same pace. The loft of the club will fly the ball over the longer fairway grass or rough and then the ball should land on the green and roll just like a putt of the same length.

■ The Accidental Champion

Lee Trevino, winner of six major titles, had a knack for playing spoiler to Jack Nicklaus, even when he wasn't trying to. Although Trevino went into the final round of the 1972 British Open at Muirfield in Scotland with the lead, he struggled through the day. Making matters worse was the inspired play of Nicklaus, who had won the year's previous two majors and was bidding for a Grand Slam. He made birdie after birdie trying to erase Trevino's six-shot margin, eventually shooting 66.

At one point, Nicklaus succeeded in taking the lead, but Trevino grabbed it back, thanks to some short-game theatrics. First, at the 16th hole, Trevino holed his bunker shot. But then he went one better, with an almost accidental hole-out from off the green at 17. In heavy rough just short of the green at the 17th hole, Trevino's pitch bounded over the green into a difficult downhill lie in the rough. Apparently disgusted and without any serious preparation, Trevino chipped again and the ball clanged off the flagstick and dropped into the hole. It marked the fourth time in the tournament

Trevino had holed a short shot from around the green. "I really wasn't trying very hard on that chip," the Merry Mex conceded after his win. "In a way, I don't feel great about it. But I hope Nicklaus wins the PGA Championship. Then, I'll be known not just as the British Open champion, but as the man who stopped the Grand Slam."

Club Selection

Why "One Swing, Many Clubs" Instead of "One Club, Many Swings"?

I believe the vast majority of recreational players choose to chip with one club, often their sand wedge, and then opt to adjust their swings to fit the length of the particular chip shot they have. There's no question this method might work for some people some of the time. I also believe that you should always consider all of your options when looking to improve. But I think I can make my case for learning to chip with a variety of clubs.

Using a sand wedge around the green makes it very difficult for the average player to get the ball to land on the green and start rolling like a putt. You have to be able to judge how far onto the green to land your shots, and that can change a great deal between a 20-foot chip and a 20-yard chip. It generally requires more practice time to discover all the different ball positions, trajectories, and swing speeds that will produce the desired-length shots. Practice time is something pros have plenty of time for, you not so much. Not only that, these subtle alterations for every situation can wreak havoc on results when the pressure is on. You want it simple when things get tense. Guessing how far on the green you should land a shot from your sand wedge introduces the kind of uncertainty that will eventually creep into your stroke.

Using a variety of clubs requires that you learn only one setup position, one ball position, one target, and one swing. If that swing doesn't get the ball to the hole with an eight-iron, a seven-iron with the same swing should do the trick.

Given how much time the average player has to work on his game, which of those sounds like the more workable option to you? Not only that, which sounds easier to you, a chipping stroke based on your putting stroke, the easiest motion in the game, or trying to hit short-game shots making mini–full swings, perhaps the most difficult move in the game?

The Three-Wood: The Ultimate Chipping Club?

Tiger Woods got some fame early in his career for occasionally bringing out his three-wood to hit chip shots around the green. A lot of people may have thought this method was a little bizarre, but I think it's a perfectly logical way to hit certain chip shots. It's a natural extension of the idea of using different clubs to hit different-length chips.

And here's a little fact you might not have known: Tiger Woods may have popularized it, but he didn't invent it. It all started on the Senior PGA Tour in the mid-1980s, and the inspiration was just the sort of frustration all recreational players experience with their own chipping games. Gardner Dickinson was the first pro I know of who used the shot, and in his case and that of many other senior players, necessity was the mother of invention. Just as putting strokes can lead to a little case of the yips as the years pile up, so too can your chipping motion, particularly on tight lies around the green. Trying to hit a sand wedge (or any club that has a significant degree of bounce on it) can be very difficult when lies are thin or tightly mown as they are on tour event courses.

Here's a breakdown of the advantages and disadvantages of chipping with your three-wood. On the plus side:

- You don't have to get the ball in the air. Hitting shots in the air requires more skill and results in greater risk, particularly for short shots.

- Again, you can use a modified putting stroke, the easiest stroke to make in the game.

- The three-wood's larger sole makes it easier for the club to glide along the ground, eliminating worry about a sharp leading edge getting stuck in the ground.

- The slight loft of the club should provide enough air time to have the ball get over the longer grass immediately in front of the ball, making it easier to maintain its speed as it starts rolling on the ground.

However, the three-wood isn't the right choice in every situation, and it's not the easiest stroke to master. Here are the negatives:

- Obviously, you can't use the three-wood if you've got to get the ball airborne over rough, traps, or any other hazard.

- Because the club is so much longer than your typical chipping club and has to be held very vertical to maximize its effectiveness, you have to choke down almost all the way past the end of your grip to the shaft. That makes for an awkward hold on the club and an unnatural motion.

- Holding the club that upright makes the sweet spot much more difficult to hit.

Knowing what it has going for it, the three-wood is a viable option, provided you've spent some time learning the technique. It's not normal, but it can be extremely effective. Don't pull it out in your next round until you've spent a few practice sessions working out the unfamiliar aspects of the stroke.

Here are the keys to executing the stroke properly:

1 Grip far enough down on the three-wood so that it feels more like the length of your putter. (To give you an idea, the average three-wood is about 42 to 43 inches long, the average putter is 34 to 35 inches long, and the length of a typical grip is about eight or nine inches.)

2 Hold the club in the middle of the left hand (more in the palm than the fingers) with the shaft angled about as upright as your putter. As with other clubs, when chipping with your three-wood, you may have to lift the heel of the club slightly off the ground to get the proper shaft angle.

3 Set your sternum, body weight, and shaft more to the left side.

4 Because you've got a longer and more unwieldy club, grip it firmly and make a stroke similar to your putting stroke. Make sure the length of your follow-through matches the length of your backswing. This will ensure that you make a solid aggressive stroke.

Uneven Lies

Just as with other short-game shots, the key to getting good results from bad lies starts and ends with your setup. Whether you've got an uphill stance or a downhill stance, the most significant change in your method is to make sure your weight counterbalances the slope. It is wise to take a practice swing to see where the club is making contact with the grass. You can then adjust to your new ball position to fit the slope. Here are some things to watch for:

1 Use more club. In other words, using a pitching wedge instead of a sand wedge allows you to swing in a comfortable speed that enables you to maintain your balance despite the awkward slope. You cannot effectively control distance and direction if you are not in balance.

2 Set your weight distribution to counterbalance the slope. In short, for an uphill shot, your weight should be concentrated on your left foot. For a downhill shot, keep your weight on your right foot. When the ball is above your

■ How to Rescue a Claret Jug

Very seldom if ever can it be said that a major championship has been won in the tournament's first round. The 1997 British Open at Royal Troon in Scotland might be one exception. The eventual champion, Justin Leonard, performed nothing short of a miracle during his back nine on the first day. With a three-club wind howling in his face, Leonard played holes 10 to 18 in an even-par 35 strokes, five better than the scoring average of the field that day. That's remarkable enough stuff, until you realize that that score was posted after he failed to reach a single green in regulation for those nine holes. His strong finish resulted in a 69, just two shots off the lead. Leonard would go on to post a final-round 65 to rally past the leader, Jesper Parnevik, and win by three shots. By the final round, it was Leonard's putting that keyed his surge to the top. His six-under round included 11 one-putt greens. But it was the saves in the first round that made the championship possible. Laughing after his first round, Leonard said, "Are there any saves? It may take a few minutes to list them all. I just stayed real patient, realized that there were some greens I wasn't going to be able to get to and tried to rely a little on my short game."

feet, your weight needs to be forward to the balls of your feet, and you need to grip down on the club. When the ball is below your feet, your weight needs to be on your heels, and you need more knee flex and a wider stance.

3 Adjust your setup position to match the bottom of your swing arc with the bottom of the ball.

Uphill: Ball played slightly forward in your stance.

Downhill: Ball played slightly back in the stance, shoulders open to the target line, and then swing along the shoulder line, left of the target.

Ball above feet: Choke down on the club, swing on a flatter plane.

Ball below feet: Add more knee bend and then maintain that angle of knee flex throughout the swing.

4 Uphill shots tend to go a little left naturally. Factor this in to your read. Also, uphill chips may require one more club than you'd use for a chip of similar length from a flat lie.

5 To avoid hitting downhill chips thin, make sure you maintain your posture throughout the stroke. One key to doing this is to keep your weight on the trailing leg. Also, focus on your swing path finishing toward the left. This automatically will get you swinging down the slope. One final guideline: Play the ball back in your stance while keeping your weight on the back foot. Swinging on an outside-to-in path helps the club move down the slope.

6 With the slopes around modern greens, occasionally you might find yourself in a position where the ball is severely above your feet. For example, you might be standing in a bunker while the ball remains perched outside the sand. In these cases, try to maintain the spacing between your hands and chest throughout the swing. That means you'll have to shorten up your grip so the club can work freely around your body. Again, expect the ball to come off the club to the left, because the slope naturally closes the club face. Aim a little right. It's also important to lower your expectations from a bad lie like this. Make your first mission to get the ball simply on the green. Then, take your chances from there. Sometimes accepting the possibility of getting up and down in three shots, and making sure that nothing worse than that happens, keeps your scoring for the whole round in better shape.

A Tricky Spot

We've all faced the unfortunate result of the ball trickling through the fringe and stopping tight against the collar. This doesn't happen more than once every three or four rounds, even to tour players, but it can be frustrating. The wonderful thing, however, is that you have so many options from this point. You can try a typical chip, perhaps opting for more loft so the club is better able to work through the taller grass behind the ball. Also, you could opt for the benefits of the large flat sole and bigger mass of your three-wood to push through the heavy grass toward your ball. There are two other nifty alternatives, as well.

Vijay Singh made an impressive birdie on the 17th hole at the 2001 Players Championship when he found his ball in this precarious position. Singh turned his putter on its side and hit the ball using the toe of his putter almost like a croquet mallet. The difficulties here are these: First, you have to make sure you have the right kind of putter to try this. It won't work with a mallet-headed putter, and is probably most effective when you have a heel-toe weighted putter like the Odyssey blades or Ping Anser–like designs. Anything else may be too difficult to maneuver. Also, you have to be able to make a fairly precise motion, otherwise the ball could bound off

the corner of the toe of your putter and away from the intended target. But with practice, the short popping stroke may be the right way to get the ball out of a tough spot.

A final method is to choose your sand wedge and try to belly the ball (right). The object is to contact the equator of the ball (not the bottom) with the leading edge of your sand wedge. Again, you want the club to be held extremely upright so the club goes through the grass slightly diagonally, rather than straight back and through. The diagonal route generates less resistance. You also could keep the hands trailing the club as it moves through the hitting area. This enables the bounce of your wedge to help get the club through the rough.

■ The Mightiest Mighty Mite of Them All

When you are routinely getting outdriven by 50 yards off the tee, you better have a good short game or you're going to have a hard time earning meal money in professional golf. Paul Runyan apparently knew this. That may be why his short game was so good. At the 1938 PGA Championship, his short game, along with his long game for that matter, were exceptionally good. Just ask Sam Snead. Snead, perhaps as long and straight a driver as there was in his era, dominated Runyan off the tee in the match-play final that year. But that's where his edge ended. Runyan, a 10-to-1 underdog in some circles, played thoughtfully to his strength, the short game, and he thwarted Snead at every turn. Runyan's 8-and-7 victory was the largest margin in PGA Championship history. Even on the par-5s, where Snead was sure to have an advantage, it was Runyan who made birdies and Snead who could only make pars. Runyan ended up shooting 67 in the morning round and a front-nine 35 before closing out Snead on the 11th hole.

Runyan later wrote in his own book just

how important his short-game prowess was, saying that he more often would hole a chip shot than leave himself two putts after chipping. "I hope you will look on the short game as I have my golfing life. I hope you will begin to regard it not so much as a defensive tool for keeping your scores from skying, but rather as an offensive weapon for beating the course and demoralizing your opponents."

A Calibration Guide to Chipping with Different Clubs

Our main goal with chipping is to get the ball rolling like a putt as quickly as possible. We are always trying to land the ball on the front of the green and then get it to roll. You will have to use much more club to hit a 45-foot chip than a 15-footer. That's why different-length chip shots require different clubs.

Here is a chart designed to show you what club to use on the basis of the ratio between the amount of carry and the amount of roll you can expect on a chip shot hit from the fairway or fringe, given normal, relatively flat ground conditions. Use this table to decide whether to change clubs, not to change your swing. For instance, suppose I'm going to carry a chip shot about four steps in the air to reach the green and I've got nine steps of green between my ball and the hole. This is a ratio of 1 part air time to 3 parts ground time. With this 1:3 ratio, the ideal club for me in this situation would be a nine-iron. A general rule for club selection is when you have a short distance between the ball and the green and a long distance between the front of the green and the hole, use a longer iron for chip shots. When the distance between the ball and the green is the same or greater than the distance between the front of the green and the hole, some type of wedge is often the best choice.

Club	Carry	Roll
Sand wedge	1 part	1 part
Pitching wedge	1 part	2 parts
Nine-iron	1 part	3 parts
Eight-iron	1 part	4 parts
Seven-iron	1 part	5 parts
Six-iron	1 part	6 parts
Five-iron	1 part	7 parts
Four-iron	1 part	8 parts
Three-iron	1 part	9 parts

CHAPTER THREE

PITCHING

▼ ▼ ▼ ▼

How to Win a Major
from the Parking Lot

It was the shot that defined the man and the career of Severiano Ballesteros. It came at the most crucial stage of his first victory in a major championship. Ballesteros was known throughout his career for his swashbuckling style and, more important, for his deft short game, but his talents were never been better displayed than during the final round of the 1979 British Open at Royal Lytham and St. Anne's in England. Just 22 years old, Ballesteros became the youngest winner of the British Open in the twentieth century when he held off the great Jack Nicklaus, Ben Crenshaw, and Hale Irwin coming down the stretch. And the key to it all was a sporty little pitch shot played from—of all places— a parking lot. It will forever be known as Seve's famous "car park shot," as the Brits like to call it, but what it really showed is that if you spend the time developing your short game, you are very much in every hole all the time, sometimes even when your ball comes to rest underneath a four-door sedan.

Here was the situation: Ballesteros held the lead coming into the treacherous back nine at Lytham, but he could feel the pressure from the Golden Bear and Gentle Ben. Still, rather than playing conservatively, the feisty Spaniard stuck to his guns and threw caution to the wind, blasting driver and scrambling for pars and birdies at every turn. In point of fact, he only managed to hit two fairways that final round. Nowhere was that swashbuckling style more in evidence than on the short 16th hole, a 353-yard par-4 where most players would comfortably hit an iron off the tee and leave themselves a comfortable wedge into the green. Ballesteros, however, eschewed the prudent play; leading by two shots, he whipped out his driver and lashed the ball far but unfortunately well off-line. The ball ended up relatively near the green but came to rest in an area fans had been using as a parking lot.

One thing needs to be cleared up: For years Ballesteros has been considered wild, and perhaps he is—but that particular play was actually disciplined. Seve clearly saw his target as the car park from the very beginning. He knew that it opened up the green and that the wind conditions were working in his favor. He also knew that he almost certainly would be left with a very playable pitch shot, his absolute strength. His 286-yard smash left him just 64 yards to the green. After pacing off the yardage, Ballesteros, undaunted, took out his wedge, the club that would come to define his game. He calculated the swing that would match the distance he had left to the pin and then made his play. He was surely staring at bogey or worse before he took the club back, and for all appearances his grip on the Open championship and the legendary claret jug seemed to be slipping away. Instead, in one miraculous swing, Ballesteros went from certain disaster to instant hero. The ball bounded onto the green and came to rest just 20 feet from the pin. The up-hill putt went into the cup for birdie. Seve had a three-shot lead and a hall-of-fame career had its first major highlight.

Maybe driver wasn't the wise play, but for Ballesteros, it made perfect sense. He knew that his short game was his backstop, that he could pitch himself out of almost any difficulty. Imagine having that kind of confidence in your ability to pitch the ball. Think it might make you play a little more confidently, might let you score a little better? A good pitch shot can save you a lot of strokes over the course of your round, even if you aren't driving it into the parking lot. Seve knew that; you should, too.

A Pitching Theory

The pitch shot may be the most difficult of the short-game shots because there are so many variables for each shot. There is the condition of the lie, which can vary from deep rough to tightly mown fairway grass. There is the angle of the lie, which can be downhill, uphill, and even sidehill. There is the ideal height of the shot, which might be a low, running type of shot just as often as a high, floating ball that stops quickly once it lands on the green. And there is the length of swing, which can be a full swing that varies in speed or a swing where the club never gets above chest level. Each pitch shot requires subtlety and great feel, but often there can be an element of speed and strength to this short-game shot. (If you've ever tried to advance a greenside shot out of thick, gnarly, U.S. Open–style rough, you know exactly what I'm talking about.)

The overriding element in any pitch shot, though, is getting the ball up into the air and over some potential trouble (a creek, a bunker, some thick rough) and onto the green. The great difficulty in pitch shots for many amateurs lies in that very notion of getting the ball into the air. Many feel the temptation to help their pitch shots get airborne. But that type of swing leads to a loss of control at best, and at worst may lead to topped or fat shots. Rely on the loft of your wedge and the speed of your swing to solve your struggles with this particular short-game shot. Just remember, if you're making good contact with your sand wedge, the ball will be launched on a trajectory angle high enough to get out of any thick grass or over just about any bunker. That's why the loft on your wedge is about six times as high as your driver. Trust your equipment, and focus on making solid contact with a downward motion, not a scooping or helping motion, at impact.

Great pitching isn't like great iron shots from the middle of the fairway. There, you get a yardage and generally make the same type of full swing you might make with any other iron to get the ball to fly the correct distance. With pitch shots, almost in every case you are making less than a full swing. That is an inexact science, and yet we have to be much more specific in our aim with a pitch shot than we are with any iron shot. In a way, great pitching asks us to marry some of the skills we use in our full swing with those we so often use in our putting games—the ability to read greens and navigate various uphill and downhill contours.

The pitch shot requires a great sense of imagination. A simple way to visualize what a pitch shot should feel like is to imagine yourself tossing the ball onto the green from where it lies with an underhanded motion, rather than hitting a golf shot. Ideally, the ball should fly along the same trajectory as that toss, and it should bounce and roll on the green with the same velocity. All that you are trying to do with your pitch shot is to re-create that feeling of tossing the ball.

The way to make that image a reality, of course, is to practice. And the first step in practice of any kind is to get grounded in the fundamentals. Some of the fundamentals we'll talk about in the next few pages may strike many of you as not so different from fundamentals of your full swing. But these basic ideas, along with some very specific ideas geared to your short game, are the foundation for building solid pitch shots. Regular practice and attention to detail as you approach these shots around the green will move you toward your goal of turning three shots into two.

Fundamentals

What is it we hate about pitch shots? Inconsistency. A fat shot on one swing followed by a thin shot on another swing. Coming up well short on one hole and then running the ball well by on another hole. The object of any short-game shot, as has been said many times, is to leave yourself a very easy and makable next shot, or, ideally, to leave yourself nothing to do at all, save for plucking your ball out of the cup. So if you want consistency in your pitching game, start by building consistency in your fundamentals.

Grip

Use the same grip you normally use for any full swing with an iron or wood. Avoid the tendency to hold the club in the palms of your hands. It's okay to grip the club more in the palms when you're putting, but for pitch shots, keep the club in your fingers. This allows the club to hinge and move freely in the swing, rotating open naturally on the backswing and closing naturally on the through swing. With the club in

■ A Miracle Save at the Masters

If there was a defining moment in the 1992 Masters Tournament, it came on the 12th hole, the insidiously difficult par-3 over Rae's Creek that can doom a player's chances on Sunday afternoon. Fred Couples looked to be that unfortunate victim when his shot to the slim 12th green drifted slightly right and hung up in the air, falling just short of the green. As the ball trickled down the bank, most observers were sure the ball would end up in the water. Incongruously, it stopped on the edge of the stream just 12 inches from the water, the result of some soft ground and and a few unmown blades of grass. That stroke of good fortune was one of the keys to Couples's winning the coveted title that year. Even the usually laconic Couples called it "the biggest break in my life."

What has often been overlooked, however, was Couples's nifty little pitch from that tricky lie, which landed safely on the green. Couples easily could have made bogey or worse from that precarious position. Instead, he softly lobbed the ball onto the green, where it stopped a few inches from the hole. He made his par and went on to stroll to a two-stroke victory. "I thought I could win if I could get past twelve," Couples said after the round. He did.

the palms, the tendency is for the club face to stay closed on the take-away, which leads to shots being pulled left. Maintain constant grip pressure for the entire swing. You should be able to hold the club in the crook of your index finger (right).

Stance

Pitch shots require control, and control starts with a narrow stance. Control also means avoiding the over-swing, and a good way to swing within yourself is to open your stance slightly to the target line. Also, keep your weight slightly on your left side. Remember, because you're not necessarily generating a lot of club-head speed you want good, controlled contact so the ball goes the distance you need at the trajectory you want. You want a narrow stance for the shorter shots and then the stance should get wider as the shots approach normal full-swing wedge distance. You want a stance more open for the shorter shots. As the shots get longer, though, your stance gets closer to square.

Ball position

Keep the ball slightly forward of your sternum (right). That puts the ball in line with where your swing should bottom out. If the ball position gets too far toward the back foot, you'll de-loft your wedge, leading to shots that

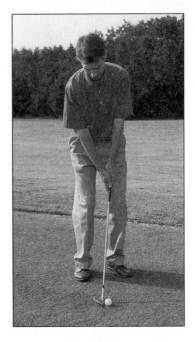

may fly lower and roll much more after landing, which makes controlling distance difficult.

Swing

Even though the pitch shot might look a great deal like your normal full swing, this shot is all about control: control of distance, control of trajectory, control of release. To build that control, there are three things to key on in your swing.

1 First, keep the pace consistent on the backswing, downswing, and follow-through. It will be that much harder to hit controlled shots if, for instance, you suddenly accelerate or slow down at impact. Remember, just let the ball get in the way of the club as it moves from one end of the swing to the other.

2 Second, concentrate on matching the length of your backswing with the length of your follow-through (above). This promotes a consistent rhythm in your pitch shots, and it cuts down on errors. If you take it back short but finish long, you'll be prone to topped shots because the bottom of your swing arc comes well after the ball. Conversely, if you take it back long but finish short, you risk hitting it fat because your swing bottoms out well before the club head reaches the ball.

3 Third, let the club face work open slightly as the club starts away from the ball. This gets the club traveling on the proper swing path for solid contact. Keeping the club face square to the target or even closed makes it more likely that the club will have to reroute to the inside on the downswing. Avoid overdoing this, though. If the club face opens too much, you're asking your hands to get too active in a short swing. That's a recipe for mis-hits and inconsistency, and even the dreaded shank. You don't want to cock the wrists at the start of your swing, either. Just let the club turn away naturally in response to the rotation of your hips and shoulders at address.

Troubleshooting

Grip pressure

To get yourself feeling the proper amount of grip pressure, first stop strangling the club. In fact, don't think of "gripping" the club, think of "holding" it.

Why proper, consistent grip pressure is so important:

- It helps tempo.
- It can eliminate excessive wrist action on the backswing and downswing. Overly involved hands and wrists are unreliable and lead to inconsistency.
- It builds the sensation of swinging the whole club back and through, not just the club head.

HOW TO FIX IT: Use a tee and a dime as reminders (see photos on page 95). First, place a tee under the last two fingers of the left hand. Then, put a dime on top of your left thumb and in between your right palm. Maintain possession of those items throughout repeated practice swings without squeezing them so hard that they leave a mark on your right fingers or hand.

Stance

Your stance is the foundation for your swing. Since the accuracy requirement with a pitch shot is much more precise than with a full swing from the tee 300 yards away or even

an iron shot from the fairway 150 yards out, you have to focus on stability. Just as you wouldn't want a lot of lower-body action with a 10-foot putt, you want your stance to support the swing without a whole lot of footwork. The pitch shot should be a turn of the upper body and shoulders and a slight hip turn combined with an arm swing. Stay steady with the lower body, keep the weight slightly forward of center, and place the feet less than shoulder width apart, slightly open to the target.

Why a proper stance is important:

- It encourages a descending blow without your having to hit down at the ball with your hands. If the weight is centered or more on the right side, your swing will bottom out too early, leading to either a topped shot or a chunk.

■ Preserving a Victory with a Recovery

Davis Love III had played 312 PGA Tour events before the big victory that so many had expected of him for so long. It finally came in August 1997 at the PGA Championship at the brutish Winged Foot Golf Club outside New York City. Winged Foot's West Course presents myriad challenges, but its greatest universally acknowledged difficulty comes around the greens where deep bunkers pinch the entrances and force elevated but soft-landing recovery shots. For Love to capture his elusive major, he would need to call on all his short-game expertise.

The deciding moment came at the difficult par-3 12th green. Love had seen his five-stroke lead trimmed to three, when he pulled his four-iron long and left into a clumpy lie with little green to work with. His nearest challenger, his playing partner, Justin Leonard, had a makable birdie putt and already there were whispers in the gallery of a two-shot swing. Love silenced the critics by softly lobbing a wedge shot up onto the green and dinging the flagstick for a tap-in par. It sealed the deal for Love and he would go on to win by five. "I think that saved the tournament for me," Love later said. "That gave me the confidence that I could get up and down from anywhere."

- A slightly narrow, open stance works to restrict the length of your swing, which helps control distance. It also encourages the shoulders to be balanced over the hips at the finish.

- A stable stance promotes accuracy by restricting leg action.

HOW TO FIX IT: Try the "stork drill" to get the proper feeling. Keep 75 percent of your weight on your left foot, dragging your right foot behind and lifting up your right heel. Making contact here requires a simple balanced swing, the best way to get more control.

Swing

It's helpful to think of matching the length of your backswing with the length of your follow-through. It builds control and helps avoid mis-hits. So when you're practicing, see if you can make swings from knee height on the backswing to knee height on the follow-through.

Why consistent swing length is important:

- Abbreviating your backswing can force you to accelerate the downswing too quickly with your arms. Your arm swing will fall out of synch with the turning of your body, altering both the direction of your shot (the club face won't be square to the target line at impact) and the distance of the hit (the club head will deliver a glancing blow because it is traveling across the target line, not along it).

- Cutting off the follow-through too quickly leads to decelerating the club head through the contact area just before and just after the ball. Shots then tend to go much higher than ideal and left of the target. That's not the control you'll need to be accurate.

- Keeping the club working in front of the body throughout the take-away, downswing, and follow-through produces a better impact position and more consistent distances.

HOW TO FIX IT: The goal is to feel the arms, not necessarily the club head, working the same length on the backswing as on the follow-through. To do this, make slow practice swings, stopping both the backswing and the follow-through at waist height. When you feel this motion becoming natural, try actually making contact with the ball. There should not be an effort to increase the speed of the swing from the initial takeaway speed. Maintain consistent pace and keep turning with the upper body. To help sense it, imagine that a string connects your sternum with the butt end of the grip. Your goal should be to keep that imaginary string taut. It won't be if your arm swing doesn't match the turning of your body.

How to Go High, Go Low, and Go in Between

Having real control of your pitching game means being able to control not only distance and direction, but also trajectory. Why would you want to hit pitch shots at different heights? First, you can use height control to take advantage of wind conditions. A low shot will penetrate a head wind without losing distance. A tail wind can help a high shot by making it fly higher and farther, but it will still land softly. Second, design features of the course may require shots of different heights. You may be well below the green and need to loft the ball high and land it soft. On the other hand, a lower shot is ideally suited when your target is a pin tucked on the back edge of the green. Trying to fly it all the way to the hole is a tough way to properly judge distance (and it brings the greater likelihood that your shot will land over the green or run through it, leaving you with another tough short-game shot). Conversely, when a pin is on the front portion of the green, a higher shot is the best way to get the ball to stop near the hole.

How to hit it low

1 Strengthen your grip by rotating both hands on the club slightly to the right.

2 Play the ball slightly back in your stance, no more than a couple of inches, and keep your hands forward of the ball so that the shaft is angled toward the target. This de-lofts the club; for example, it will give the trajectory of your wedge the trajectory of a seven-iron. Playing the ball back also closes your shoulders to the target line at address.

3 Depending on which club you're pitching with, expect the ball to roll at least twice as far as the distance it travels through the air.

4 Because you are de-lofting your club, length of swing is shorter (see photos on page 99).

How to hit it medium high

1 Your grip is neutral, with the V's on your hands pointing toward your inside right shoulder. Position the ball in the center of your stance.

2 Keep your hands slightly ahead of the ball position, but even with your belly button. This setup uses the club's true loft.

3 The pace of the swing is unforced, usual.

How to hit it high

1 The grip is weaker than normal. Your hands are rotated slightly toward the target. This opens the face, which adds loft at impact.

2 Your shoulders are open to the target line.

3 The ball will be played forward of center in your stance.

4 At address, your hands are slightly behind the club head, but still even with the belly button.

5 The ball position is slightly forward, even with the big toe of the front foot.

6 Because of the increase in loft, you'll need a longer swing to make the ball go the same distance.

Bear in Mind

Most pitch shots are shots of precision and indecision. Viewed that way, they should be avoided whenever possible. Let me explain. We all know we're going to miss some greens during a round of golf, maybe a lot of greens, even. And sometimes your recovery shot is going to have to be a pitch shot where less than a full swing is required. That's fine. What causes problems is when you lay up short of a green intentionally but still leave yourself an in-between pitch shot. Let me assure you, even the best pros don't relish a 40- or 50-yard shot. Why? Because a half- or three-quarter swing makes it difficult to accurately gauge distance. It also makes it difficult to put enough spin on the ball to get it to stop

■ Watson's Wondrous Wedge

Almost since its inception, the U.S. Open has prided itself on being the ultimate test of ball striking. It is a tournament that seems to demand fairways and greens from its winner. But so often the truly memorable moments at this championship have been the recovery shots made after poorly played full swings. Such most certainly was the case at the 1982 U.S. Open at Pebble Beach. Tom Watson, playing a few groups behind Jack Nicklaus, had battled for the lead throughout that final round. At Pebble's bullish par-3 17th hole, Watson found his ball in the deep rough less than 10 feet from the green, which was by all accounts wickedly fast. He was staring at an almost certain bogey. Or so the world thought.

While Jack Nicklaus was being interviewed as the almost certain U.S. Open champion, Watson studied the shot with his longtime caddie, Bruce Edwards. Finally, he took his sand wedge and Edwards exhorted him to "get it close." Watson was nonplussed. "I'm not gonna get it close," he growled back. "I'm gonna make it." Watson then proceeded to fulfill the prophecy, laying open his sand wedge and plopping the ball onto the firm green, where it bounded into the hole in the blink of an eye. Said Watson's playing partner, Bill Rogers, "You could hit that chip a hundred times, and you couldn't get close to the pin, much less in the hole." "A thousand times," corrected Nicklaus. But for Watson, the momentous wedge shot— part chip shot, part pitch shot, part lob shot— wasn't blind luck. "I've practiced that shot for hours, days, months, and years," Watson said that famous Sunday in 1982. "It's a shot you have to know if you're going to do well in the Open. That shot at seventeen meant more to me than any other golf shot I ever made."

where you want it. Pitch shots are a necessary part of the game, but if you have the option, always leave yourself a full swing into the green. That means, for example, that on a long par-5, you don't want to leave an in-between distance for your approach shot. Lay back so you have a comfortable full swing into the hole. I'm all for getting a solid short game—but just don't force yourself to hit unnecessarily difficult shots when they can be avoided.

Some Reminders

1 No matter whether you are making a full swing or an in-between swing for your pitch shot, a ball hit from the rough generally will run a greater distance after it lands than a shot hit from the fairway. The longer the shot to the green, generally the more it will run after hitting the green.

2 Two is the bare minimum number of wedges you should carry. I recommend three wedges for most players. Although some tour players have gravitated to carrying four wedges, I'd suggest three is plenty. Now, which three wedges you carry is up to you. Before you decide, you need to determine how and where you typically play. If you often leave yourself 100 yards to the hole, it would be ideal to have a club that covers that distance. For many average players, this means that a wedge with a loft between that of your pitching wedge (approximately 48 degrees) and your sand wedge (approximately 56 degrees) might be the key wedge. On the other hand, you may play a course with many elevated greens with deep bunkers. A greenside club that has more loft, like a 60-degree lob wedge, may be more useful than a wedge that covers your in-between distances. If you decide this is the proper club for you, I'd take a look at modifying the lofts of your other wedges. You might want to go with a 50-degree pitching wedge and a 55-degree sand wedge.

3 A big temptation average players must resist is the urge to try to "help" your pitch shots into the air by making a scooping motion. If you do this you're more likely to top the ball or hit it fat, not get it up into the air. Work on trusting the loft of your wedge. A good trick to convince you the loft of your wedge is sufficient is to take your wedge and step on the club face so the shaft is angled toward your target. That shaft angle matches the trajectory of your wedge.

4 On the backswing you have to let the club open naturally and the wrists hinge naturally (below, right). You don't want to bring the club straight back and low to the ground to start the swing. This would not keep the arms swinging in front of the body and allow the club face to open naturally. Because the wedges are shorter clubs and you'll be standing closer to the ball, your swing path will be naturally steeper than it would be with a wood shot and you'll be standing closer to the ball. But this is a natural position, achieved without a single training aid.

5 Occasionally teachers will say that pitch shots are like "pinching" the ball between the club head and ground. I know what they mean, but this image can be confusing. It ingrains the idea of trying to be too precise with the club face at impact. That can causes too much ball orientation, instead of being focused on the target or your swing. In truth, because of the bounce angle on the sole of your sand wedge (due to the fact that the trailing edge of the sole is lower than the leading edge), you can actually sometimes hit a good five inches behind the ball and get good results in many situations.

6 Many amateurs become overly immobile when they prepare for pitch shots. They realize how important precision is in greenside shots but they overdo it. Concentrating on not moving takes away some of your natural feel. Feel free to let your legs and knees move slightly during the swing. Don't worry. You've already got built-in restrictions to your swing: a shorter club, a narrow stance, and an open stance. Letting the legs and lower body move freely, not wildly, should produce a more reliable contact.

7 Practice makes perfect. But don't get in a rut. Practicing one distance from one lie won't be helpful in on-course situations because you'll never have that same exact distance. Instead, practice different pitching distances, and rotate through those pitching distances during a typical practice session. If you have the luxury, I'd even try going out on the course before dark one night and dropping practice balls in different lies and at different yardage around each green, anywhere within 40 yards of the putting surface. See how often you can get up and down.

- To feel a one-piece movement back and through the swing without excessive wrist action, extend your right index finger down the back of the shaft. Your hands have to stay very passive if you're going to make good contact.

- Hit practice shots with your hands separated slightly (about a quarter of an inch). This will keep your elbows from locking up and it also allows the club to hinge on your backswing and finish.

Special Situations

How to play a short pitch from heavy rough

Being successful from the deep grass requires confidence, good fortune, and solid technique. That was how Tom Watson holed a crucial greenside pitch on the 71st hole and went on to win the 1982 U.S. Open at Pebble Beach. Here are the keys to focus on when your ball nestles down in some deep grass:

1 Open the club face at address and grip the club slightly more firmly than normal. This will help the club resist twisting, which could close the face once the club head gets into the deep rough.

2 Make a longer backswing than such a distance would normally require. This will help you generate the club-head speed you'll need to get the club moving through the deep grass.

■ Singh's Sneaky-Good Short Game

Vijay Singh is known as a player who loves to work on his full swing. He still hits practice shots with his driver out on the practice range until it gets dark, much as he did in his early days when he was the teaching pro at the Keningau Club in the rain forests of Borneo. But when he won the 2000 Masters—where his long shots, not surprisingly, were powerful and spectacular—it was the short game that saved him when all could have been lost. Holding a two-shot lead, Singh found trouble at Augusta National's difficult par-4 11th hole, hitting his second shot into the greenside pond. Taking a careful drop to the side of the green, Singh lofted a sporty little pitch that checked up four feet from the hole. He drained the putt for a bogey, when a double bogey or worse was a possibility. Now, with a single-stroke lead, Singh again had to rely on his short game. His shot to the tricky par-3 12th hole went well over the green and kicked off a bank and into a back bunker. Facing an explosion shot that if even slightly mis-hit could roll off the green and into the greenside stream,

Singh calmly blasted his shot to two feet. His margin maintained, Singh rallied with fine play down the stretch to win by a commanding three shots. "I was so focused on what I was doing," the champion said. "It feels wonderful."

3 Play the ball forward in the stance. This allows the swing path to be steep to help the club get down toward the ball. Make sure to swing on an outside-to-in path and keep your weight on your lead foot.

4 As the club moves through the grass, hold the club face open so that it doesn't close too much before impact. It may close slightly because of the deep grass, but that closing will actually bring the club face closer to square to the target at impact. A closed club face will produce a low left shot, generally not a good way to get your pitch shots close to the hole.

5 Remember, the ball is going to run a fair amount after it lands. That means you should aim for your shot to land well short of the flag whenever possible.

How to play from a tight lie

With the developments in agronomy these days, it is not unusual to find your ball near the green yet resting on some fairly well trimmed bit of grass. You will find many tight lies in the so-called chipping areas in the runoffs around greens, where the putting surface is often significantly elevated from the area around the green, yet the grass is often cut to fairway height or even shorter. These are typically the conditions around green complexes modeled after those found at Pinehurst No. 2.

In these situations, there certainly are safer options than trying a lofted pitch shot. If you have the choice, always opt for the putter or even a five- or six-iron chip-and-run sort of shot. But if you don't have a lot of green to work with or there is something nasty between your ball and the putting surface (a bunker, a stream, some heavy grass), the pitch is your best choice—provided, of course, you've developed some confidence through practice.

Here are some guidelines to help you get the ball up where you want it:

1 Consider club selection. From a very tight lie or hard pan, the sand wedge may work against you. The bounce in the sole of your sand wedge (the way the trailing edge is lower than the leading edge) may cause the club's trailing edge to contact the ground too early and the club could skid or hop along the ground, leading to fat or skulled shots. If you have the availability, a 60-degree wedge with no bounce is the ideal club from a tight lie.

2 Your setup at address should be normal, with the following variations: Use a slightly weaker grip than normal (hands rotated more toward the target). Also, stand a little closer to the ball. This helps eliminate excessive wrist action from your stroke (which could lead to poor contact) and puts a smaller piece of the club on the ground. The shoulders are level and aimed slightly left, which will result in the club face open at impact.

3 Make the normal backswing and as you swing through, allow the club to finish with the toe pointing up. This finish keys good balance by keeping the chest on top of the hips. Good balance is essential for solid contact.

4 As a reminder, focus on the handle pointing at the middle of the body throughout the swing. This should keep the club moving on the downswing, avoiding decelerating the club head on the downswing or simply not moving the hands and arms fast enough. You can't expect to make consistently solid contact if the body is outracing the arms on a short pitch shot.

Things to watch out for

Getting too ball-oriented

It is a scary lie. Staring at it only ingrains that idea, and it doesn't help you execute the shot. To avoid becoming overly ball-conscious, brush the ground with your practice swings to ingrain the proper feel, set up to the ball, take one last look, and then swing—without hesitation.

Ball too far back, hands too far forward

This setup ensures only one thing: you've de-lofted your sand wedge, and will hit a much lower shot than expected. This setup also makes aiming difficult because shots tend to go well left of the intended path. If the ball is closer to your right big toe than to your left big toe, you're probably playing the ball too far back. Inside the left heel is always a solid guideline. But remember, with the narrow stance in your pitch setup, the ball may sometimes look as though it's in the middle or back portion of your stance when it's not.

Overaccelerating

We're all a little bit afraid of quitting on a shot. Decelerating is a problem, but overdoing it is, too. Excessive downswing acceleration can lead to only one result, an unreliable move and poor tempo—not what you want for the more precise shots. Acceleration should never be forced. I've never seen a pro player of any caliber, where the length of his follow-through was longer than that of his backswing.

Too much wrists

By overdoing your backswing with wrist action, you can get the handle of the club working in the opposite direction from the club head and at a different speed. To combat this problem, place your hands together and swing them back and forth. You should notice the lack of hand action, and how the elbows fold, just as in every other swing.

How to Hit the Flop Shot

The flop shot is a contradiction. You swing the club very fast in hopes of hitting it very short. That is a very difficult thing to do. But because players like Tiger Woods and Phil Mickelson have shown us you can hit high soft shots around the green, the flop shot has become extremely popular. In fact, Mickelson was photographed on the cover of *Golf Digest* several years ago hitting a flop shot backward over his head and onto the green from a severely sloping lie. When it comes to average golfers, however, I think that those with a little bit of ability resort to this shot much too often. It is a very difficult shot and the downside is often much greater than any potential upside. There are some things every golfer should be aware of before the flop shot becomes a regular part of his résumé.

1 The flop shot is a glancing blow, somewhat similar to a bunker shot. Therefore, you have to swing much harder and longer than the distance might indicate for a normal pitch shot.

2 The club face should be slightly open (the face looks more toward the sky than down the target line), and so should your stance.

3 The ball should be positioned forward of your normal ball position (slightly ahead of your sternum). A general guideline is to play the ball even with the big toe on your left foot.

4 In the flop-shot swing, you want to generate a significant amount of club-head speed, which means you need to make a full backswing and finish. The club head should pass the hands just after impact, and the club should get above your shoulders on the follow-through. The swing path should be more outside to in, rather than straight at the target.

5 The flop shot should be your last resort, not your first option. Why? Because a normal pitch should put the ball on the green within two-putt range. Because the likelihood of executing the flop shot well is rare, you could just as easily leave the ball right where it is or hit it thin and have it sail well over the green. Generally, you should use the flop shot *only* if you have sufficient practice time and a high degree of confidence with it. Use it only when you have to hit a high, short shot to a pin set tight against the edge of the green or a severe slope.

The best advice I can give regarding the flop shot? Don't put yourself in a situation where you have no other option. In other words, avoid missing the green in a spot where there is no other play. Usually that means aiming away from a pin that is tucked in a corner. Sometimes the best play is to aim for the center of the green, regardless of how far it is from the hole. Besides, you've probably been practicing your putting much more than your flop shots. Take your chances with two-putting from 40 feet instead of attempting a high soft short shot that would be a struggle for even the best players in the world.

CHAPTER FOUR

BUNKER PLAY

▼ ▼ ▼ ▼

The Most Important Golfer in History— It's Not Who You Think

The debate as to who is the greatest golfer ever may rage on for decades to come. There's no question that solid cases can be made for Tiger Woods, Jack Nicklaus, Ben Hogan, and Bobby Jones. And who knows what superstar may be waiting in the wings as we speak? I couldn't even begin to decide among those four legends. Woods with his power, dominance, and great sense of theater. Nicklaus with his unmatched concentration, unfailing course management skills, and amazing staying power through three decades. Hogan with his machinelike intensity, diligence on the practice tee, and uncanny knack for hitting the perfect shot at the perfect moment. Or Jones for his majestic flowing swing, effortless grace, and incredible 1930 Grand Slam season.

All of these players stand above the rest on their own plateau. Choosing one of them over the others would be unfair, in addition to being impossible. Yet for all their achievements, for their glittering character and singleness of purpose, they all must take a backseat to one other legend in his own right. Even as great as they all are, Woods, Nicklaus, Hogan, and Jones never impacted the average golfer the way Gene Sarazen still does every day and in every place golf is played. How so? Simple. Gene Sarazen invented the sand wedge. Without it, all of us would be playing tennis.

Sarazen was, of course, a brilliant player in his day. He won two major championships before his twenty-first birthday, in 1922. And we all know about his famous double eagle at the 15th hole in the final round of the 1935 Masters, which led to his victory there in a playoff. But it's what happened during the winter months of 1931–32 that most people, including Sarazen—a man who, we shouldn't forget, won a total of seven major titles in his career—consider his most important achievement. Tinkering in his golf shop and experimenting in a backyard bunker at his home at the New Port Richey Country Club in Florida, Sarazen worked on solving the nagging problem in his game: bunker play.

Building on a principle of flight he had learned while taking flying lessons from the millionaire aviator Howard Hughes, Sarazen took a pitching club and fashioned a wider flange on the bottom of the club. The result was a sole where the trailing edge would actually contact the sand first, gliding along the sand, taking a shallow divot and forcing the ball up and out of the bunker. Sarazen referred to it as a club that "would drive the ball up as he drove the club head down." Soldering lead to the bottom of his club and then going out to the bunker, Sarazen hit thousands of shots. The new club worked, and, more important, Sarazen's bunker method improved, too.

That 1932 season, Sarazen stormed through golf's two premier championships, the U.S. and British Opens. He won the British at Prince's with a 13-under score that broke the old record by two shots. Later, at the U.S. Open at Fresh Meadow, Sarazen again set a scoring record and played the final 28 holes in an amazing 100 strokes. His final-round 66 stood as the lowest final-round score by an Open winner for 28 years.

If after hearing all that, you don't think bunker play is worth the time and effort, you haven't been paying attention. But if you do get solid in this part of your short game, don't thank me, thank Mr. Sarazen. More important, thank yourself, because being a good bunker player is well within the reach of any player who makes time to practice and learns just how easy this shot can be.

A Bunker-Play Theory

Almost from the day Mr. Sarazen invented the sand wedge and perfected the art of using it, we have heard how easy it is to play shots out of a bunker. Strangely, there is probably no single situation that causes more apprehension and uncertainty in the mind of the average golfer than the bunker shot. It seems illogical. Easy but feared? How can it be both? Well, the short answer is that for most professionals, bunker shots are easy because there often is no uncertainty. In general, a pro feels that the bottom line is that no matter how poorly he swings he will get the ball out of the bunker, on the green and moving toward the pin. Think of it this way: the object of the bunker shot is to blast the ball out of the sand by contacting a "divot" of sand behind the ball with enough force to expel both the sand and the ball out of the bunker. In other words, hitting a bunker shot correctly means missing the ball entirely. Pros realize that in most bunker situations they don't have to be precise to get the result they're looking for. Essentially, a player can miss the ball to a variety of degrees and in all cases the ball will end up in roughly the same position. If he hits well behind the ball it may not fly very far or high, but it will roll a good bit after landing. On the other hand, if the player's swing contacts the ground a little close to the ball, it will fly out of the bunker on a higher trajectory, but when it lands it will stop more quickly. All other things being equal, those two very different types of misses could very well produce shots that end up traveling the same distance.

So why do average players often feel so uncertain if they find themselves in a bunker? I don't really know, but I imagine one possible answer is that they feel like the man who has driven an automatic-transmission car his entire life and then finds himself handed the keys to a rental car with a standard transmission. Though he probably understands the basic principles of clutch in, shift to new gear, clutch out, he is not very comfortable executing the maneuver in a practical situation. That is what happens in a bunker. We all know you hit behind the ball, the sand flies out, and the ball follows. What we don't know, and what we don't get fundamentally solid in, is the idea of executing that concept.

Being a competent bunker player means two things. First, you have to understand how the shot will work. Second, you have to learn to put yourself in the proper setup position to execute the swing in an uncomplicated manner. Having some measure of success in the bunker shouldn't cause any greater degree of mental anguish than making contact with the ball with your putter. So, focus on setup, understand what type of swing works best, and then simply execute it freely. Bunkers may be a hazard, but they need not be a permanent impediment to improving your score.

Bunker Fundamentals

I'm not going to mince words. When it comes to bunker shots, the pros are basically right. Bunker shots on the most basic level should be exceptionally easy. Let me repeat that: bunker shots on the most basic level should be exceptionally easy. Moreover, there are things you can do that don't involve great swing speed or massive upper-body strength or a tremendous sense of touch or timing that will make you a more successful bunker player right now. In short, success in the bunker begins and ends with the setup.

1 Ball position is slightly forward of normal, even with the left armpit (right). Remember, the object of the bunker-shot swing is to contact the sand before the ball. Having the ball position forward ensures the weight distribution, angle of attack on the downswing, swing path, and contact point all will be ideal. In short, your setup sets up a successful bunker shot.

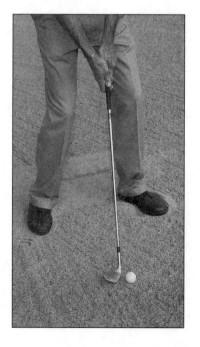

2 The stance is open to the target line to a degree

■ Tiger Stays Tough to the End

Even those with a lot of perspective might have a hard time deciding which was the most important shot of the epic final-round struggle between Tiger Woods and Bob May at the 2000 PGA Championship. Any number of putts stand out: Woods's gutty par save on the 15th hole, his nervy six-footer on the 72nd hole that forced the playoff, and of course his electrifying 20-footer on the 16th hole that gave him a one-stroke lead in the playoff. Those were all big moments in Tiger's victory, but it was his last swing of the day that was at least as crucial as any of those putts. Having chopped his way up the 18th hole, Woods found himself bunkered and facing a long blast to the hole. His lead was just one shot, and while his worthy opponent Bob May was not certain to make birdie, Woods knew that getting up and down was key to his having a chance to win his second straight PGA Championship. Woods made a very difficult shot look easy, as he often does. Although he could have left the ball in the bunker or put himself in three-putt range on the topsy-turvy green, Woods nipped the ball neatly up and out of the bunker to within two feet, thus securing his third major championship in a row.

consistent with the length of shot. In other words, a shorter shot generally requires a more open stance, whereas a longer shot requires a stance only slightly open from your usual position. More important, pay attention to ball position. On shorter shots, play the ball forward of the left heel. As the shots get longer, play the ball progressively further back toward the middle of your stance.

3 You weight should favor the target foot. The torso stays over the lead foot throughout the swing. If you lean back on your right side, you risk the swing's bottoming out too early. When that happens, either you will hit too far behind the ball, or, worse, your sand wedge will skip through the sand and contact the ball with a thin, skulled shot that flies over the green.

NOTE: To avoid the tendency to lean back, make sure the ball position is forward, not toward the middle.

4 Dig your feet into the sand until you are stable; the feet stay in the sand throughout the swing. A general rule of thumb is to twist your feet into the sand until the level of the sand is above the depth of the heels of your shoes.

5 Line up the club face toward the hole, but laid open, again to a degree that matches the length and type of shot to be played (see photo on page 121). But be careful. If you lay the club face open excessively, you'll negate the benefits of the bounce angle on the sole of your sand wedge. You'll also force yourself to make a much longer swing than is necessary, increasing the precision you'll need to get the ball to go the proper distance.

Bunker Swing

The perfect bunker swing essentially is no different from your normal swing. However, because you have aligned your body and stance open to the target line (and because your club face is open, too), your swing will appear to be an outside-to-in motion. Of course, in terms of the relationship of your swing to the ball and target line, it is an outside-to-in motion, because you are cutting across the line at impact. But remember your address position is well open to the target line to begin with. In truth, in relation to your body and shoulder and stance, your swing is on the same plane, going back and coming forward, just as it should be. Simply swing along your shoulder line, keeping the club moving on the same plane. If you try to swing in an outside-to-in plane after having set up open to the target line, you'll make a much more glancing blow and the ball will not be propelled the proper distance.

Here are a few bunker-swing tips:

1 Swing along the line of your shoulders. You are obviously trying to get the ball to fly down the target line, but because you are attempting to do so by displacing sand, you will be successful only if you swing on an outside-to-in path. In other words, swinging straight toward the target is likely to result in the leading edge of your sand wedge digging into the sand far short of the ball instead of gliding through it. This often ends up leaving the ball still in the bunker. You don't want to dig a hole in the sand with your wedge. You want to displace a shallow swath of sand, and you want to keep the club head moving.

2 Concentrate on a full follow-through. The club head absolutely must keep moving through the sand if the ball is to get out of the bunker.

3 There are several good rules of thumb for how hard to swing. The teacher John Elliott once remarked in *Golf Digest* that the ideal "divot" of sand for a typical greenside bunker shot should be about the size of a shoeprint. He said, "On bunker explosion shots, my ideal divot is exactly the same size as my shoe. I take a size-ten divot. I'm not kidding! In fact, your divot should also be about the same width as your shoe, and it should be about as deep as the sole of your shoe. In my case, that's a D-width divot and a sole about five eighths of an inch deep." Generally speaking, think of your bunker-shot swing as being three times as hard as you'd swing from a normal clean lie. In other words, if you've got a 10-yard bunker shot, it might be helpful to imagine swinging as hard as you would for a 30-yard wedge shot from a normal lie. You won't make the proper divot, though, unless you concentrate on keeping the club moving well into your follow-through.

4 Generally, the club should be working up more on the backswing because of your setup position. Overall, the bunker swing is on a steeper angle than a normal swing. Remember, you're not trying to pick the ball cleanly; you're trying to do what Mr. Sarazen set out to do when he invented the sand wedge—hit down (into the sand, behind the ball) to make the ball go up.

5 This is a swing made almost exclusively with the arms and upper body. That means no leg action until you get into your follow-through. Simply focus on keeping the weight over your left side and then swing the club up, bring it down, and swing it through to the finish.

6 Be sure to make the swing a consistent pace (see photo sequence). Avoid a slow take-away and then an accelerated downswing. Moving the club down too fast often results in overactive hands that cause the leading edge of your wedge to strike the sand too early and dig into the ground, not slide through the top layer of the sand. Give yourself enough backswing to help you generate enough speed on the downswing to blast through the sand and put the ball on the green.

■ The Unexpected Winner

Bob Tway was not supposed to win the 1986 PGA Championship. Sure, he had had a phenomenal year and was coming into the PGA with three wins, but it was the man paired with Tway in the final pairing of the final round at Inverness Club in Ohio who was drawing all the attention. Greg Norman had nearly won all three of the year's previous major titles, but had claimed only the British Open at Turnberry. Now he was again poised for victory in the PGA.

On the short par-4 18th hole, Tway left his approach short of the flag and in a bunker. He had little green to work with, and nearly everyone watching the proceedings assumed that the worst Norman could do would be to end up in another playoff. Instead, Tway executed as pure a short bunker shot as has ever been hit; he blasted the ball just over the high lip of the front bunker and then leaped for joy as the ball trickled into the hole. Norman, thoroughly disheartened, actually ended up bogeying the hole to lose by two strokes. But for Tway, it was a stirring finish, the first time anyone had ever birdied the final hole to win a PGA Championship. "For something like that to happen on the eighteenth hole, it's just indescribable," Tway said. "I may never hit a shot like that again in my whole life." He didn't—and no one else has either.

Bunker Tips

Here's a quick checklist for troubleshooting your play in the sand:

1 Keep that weight toward the target throughout the swing. If you lean back, you're going to hit the sand too far behind the ball.

2 When playing a bunker shot, focus on the ball, not the sand behind it.

3 If your setup is correct (ball equal with left toe, club, stance, shoulders open to the target line), you will automatically hit behind the ball.

4 When the ball is sculled over the green, it's never because you have swung too hard. It's also likely that it's not because you've contacted the ball before the sand. Rather, it's because you've tried to scoop the ball out at the bottom of your swing. This often causes your sand wedge to bounce off the sand well before the ball and you hit the ball thin with the leading edge of your sand wedge.

5 When a ball is left in the bunker, the golfer usually has tried to take too much sand before reaching the ball. That's one danger of swinging solely with the arms—you are likely to drive the club head into the sand. Remember to allow your torso to turn in the follow-through.

6 Your feet and shoulders are aligned left of the target. Although the temptation is to swing toward the target, make sure you swing along your shoulder line. The open club face will counteract the open stance to get the ball moving toward your target.

7 Don't choke down on the shaft. That shortens the diameter of your swing and decreases swing speed, making it that much more difficult to generate enough force to get the ball to go the proper distance. Shortening up on the club also brings up the possibility of hitting the shot thin, or worse, contacting the ball first, not the sand. Remember, the object with a bunker shot is to contact the sand, not the ball. It's like the great teacher Claude Harmon, Sr., once said of bunker shots: "Hit the big ball, not the little ball." The "big ball" he was talking about? Why, the earth, of course.

Bad Lies

As much as we hope for a relatively flat, clean lie in the bunker, just as in the fairway, it rarely happens that way. Instead, we're bound to face a slew of unusual situations that can make our stay in the bunker less pleasant and perhaps a little longer than we'd prefer. Here's what to watch out for and how to beat it in the bunker:

The buried lie

It's easy to see how this sand-trap situation got its name, but that's about the only thing easy with this lie. No one likes to have a shot when the ball is buried, even the pros. In fact, the outcome of the 1961 Masters was determined by such a lie. The great Arnold Palmer was leading by one when he played the final hole, and it appeared that the fan favorite might claim his third green jacket. A supporter even congratulated him as he was walking up the 18th fairway. Too soon, it turns out. Palmer's high approach shot leaked into the right bunker on the fly, becoming slightly buried in the fluffy sand. Palmer misplayed the shot and sculled the ball into a bunker on the other side of the green. Three more shots and he had lost the Masters by a single shot. What did Palmer do wrong, aside from let down his guard a little bit? He tried to play a buried-lie bunker shot the way he played a normal bunker shot. The fact is, you have to change your approach with a buried lie. Here's what to do:

1 Instead of thinking of blasting the ball out, with a buried lie you have to think of gouging the ball from the bunker. That means instead of using the bounce angle on your sand wedge and letting the sole glide through the sand, you have to contact the sand with the leading edge of your wedge first, not the trailing edge.

2 When the lie is bad, you need to position the ball back a little more, instead of playing the ball forward, as with a typical bunker shot.

3 Because this is a gouge more than a swing, you don't want to open up the club face. That leads to a skulled shot because the ball lies below the level of the sand. The club most likely will skip through the sand and contact the ball along its equator. Instead, keep the club face square to the target as you would for a normal lie in the fairway.

4 With a buried lie, focus on a point about an inch behind the ball. If it's the special type of buried lie called a fried egg, in which the ball is encircled by a small crater of sand, focus on a point along the outside edge of the "white" of the egg.

5 The swing is different, too. For a buried lie, you have to think of burying your club in the sand behind the ball without any appreciable follow-through. That sort of energy should force the ball out.

6 As with typical bunker shots, the key is the setup. With the ball back, your hands ahead of the ball, and your chest and upper-body weight forward of the ball, you will make a swing that is more up and down than around your body. (Note: For many high-handicappers, this type of swing is natural, so don't feel that you have to manufacture a completely different swing.) Maintain the weight and hand position throughout the swing.

7 Remember, in this situation, your only option is to get the ball out of the bunker. The ball will come out with little or no spin and the ball is likely to react as if you had thrown it onto the green from the edge of the bunker. It will roll at least three times farther than it flies through the air, probably more. Calculate that extra roll when you pick your target.

Long Bunker Shots

Often, the big problem with hitting a really bad shot is having to get yourself out of the trouble you've just put yourself into. That's especially true in the case of long bunker shots. It's difficult enough simply to pop a ball out of a bunker, but to have to launch it over 15, 20, or even 30 yards of sand and green requires a combination of strength and skill and a little foresight. But it's not impossible. In fact, it might even be a little easier than you think.

1 First, if the amount of swing and pace required for a bunker shot is equal to three times what might be required for a similar-length shot hit from a clean lie in the fairway, and if you figure your maximum distance from the fairway with a sand wedge to be about 100 yards, then right away you can see that a 30-yard bunker shot could easily require your maximum swing with a sand wedge. Therefore, make an aggressive move on the ball. Make sure you follow through fully and allow the club face to close naturally after contact as it would on any other full shot.

2 Second, get your setup working for you. Keep the ball well forward so you'll have confidence you'll contact the sand first. Keep the club face open, so your wedge will glide through the sand. This is crucial, especially when you're making a hard, full swing. If the club face isn't open, it could bounce along the sand and hit the ball thinly and the ball would bound well over the green.

3 Make a long finish, allowing the club face to rotate closed into the follow-through. Keeping this in mind will help you generate the extra speed you'll need to propel the ball out of the bunker.

■ Struggling to Survive

In professional golf, there may be few milestones as important as winning your first major championship. Especially when you're trying to hold on to your lead coming down the stretch. Especially when you haven't been playing well the last few holes. That's exactly where Andy North found himself at the 1978 U.S. Open at the Cherry Hills Country Club outside of Denver. North had led by as many as five strokes during the final round, and even when he reached the 18th tee, his lead was still a comfortable two shots. Playing safely just short of the greenside bunker in two strokes, North had just a little flick of a wedge shot and two putts to secure his title.

But in golf, especially in the short game, what looks easy often isn't. As North would later admit, he got "just a little too cute" with his pitch shot, and instead of landing on the green, the ball plopped into the bunker. Now, in order to win the major championship that had seemed a sure thing moments before, North would have to get up and down from the deep greenside bunker with the wind howling at gusts of 35 miles per hour. He steadied himself, blasted out cleanly to four feet, and then, backing away from his putt twice, finally holed the winning putt.

4 Consider that there are two ways to be successful with the long bunker shot. You can contact the sand very close to the ball and the ball will fly in the air farther, but will land with a lot of spin so it will stop shorter. Or you can contact the sand well behind the ball and the ball won't fly as far but will land with little or no spin and roll a substantial distance. In either case, the ball should travel the same total distance.

5 If you're facing a shot longer than 30 yards, consider using a nine-iron instead of your sand wedge. The extra length in the shaft and the lower loft of the club will let you swing a little easier. Keep the same setup (ball and weight forward; club face slightly open).

Short Bunker Shots

Occasionally, you will miss your approach by just a little bit—and end up in the worst place you can be. It's what the pros call getting short-sided, and it's about as much fun as getting short-sheeted. Say the pin is tucked on the right edge of the green, just to the left of a big, deep bunker. If you miss your shot right of the flag, odds are you'll end up in the bunker and you'll face as difficult a shot as there is to get up and down: a short shot with little green to work with that must stop quickly. The options on what to do in this situation are basically two: (1) Hit a conservative shot that gets the ball out of the bunker, but leaves a long, difficult putt. In almost every instance, this is the best option, because for the most part it takes double and triple bogey out of the equation. But there is a second choice. (2) Make a special setup and swing that if executed precisely will get the ball up quickly and stop it even quicker. This is a risky play and is best left to better players, but here are some tips to make it happen:

1 Make sure the club face is open, perhaps slightly more than on a normal-length bunker shot.

2 Keep the grip weaker than normal, with your right hand turned slightly more toward the target. A weaker grip levels the shoulders, allowing a steeper angle of attack, which should help the ball get up in the air quicker. It also helps keep the club head open as it moves through the sand.

3 The ball is played forward, just off the left big toe. This lets the club head work under the ball and allows for a more glancing blow to the sand.

4 Make an aggressive swing with a fairly full backswing and an abbreviated follow-through. To get the high, soft, short shot, feel the handle of the club point to your belly button at contact and into the follow-through. This gets the club head moving quicker than the grip. The result is added loft and increased bounce, two keys to hitting a higher shot.

Uneven Lies

Ideally, you're going to get a flat lie in the bunker. Realistically, that's not always going to happen. In truth, it may not even happen half of the time. Here's how to handle those uneven lies in the bunkers.

Uphill lie

First, angle the line of your shoulders to match the slope. (With an uphill stance, your left shoulder will be higher than your right.) Angling the shoulders probably puts you in position to take the proper amount of sand, as opposed to having your sand wedge dig into the bunker. Second, you'll want to open the club face just slightly. Third, make an even longer swing than for a normal bunker situation. Even a properly executed shot from this situation is going to fly higher and shorter than normal. So make a longer swing to get the ball to go the proper distance.

Downhill lie

Again, match the angle of your shoulder line to the lay of the land. (Downhill means your right shoulder is higher than your left.) Play the ball slightly back of its normal bunker position, more toward the middle of your stance. But the real key to this situation—and the real difficulty— is avoiding making a big follow-through. I know that's contrary to the normal bunker-shot thinking, but trying to make a full follow-through with a downhill lie often results in losing your balance and having your weight shift to your back foot. That means you'll take too much sand and leave the ball in the bunker. The other key is to keep your shoulders at an angle that matches the downward slope of the bunker throughout the whole swing. If you're not totally committed to this shot, consider an easier option by playing right or left of your target. Then, try to get up and down from there. It sounds difficult, but it's much better than being tentative, failing to execute the bunker shot properly, and having to face the same situation again.

Ball above feet

Keep the ball centered in your stance, but make sure you grip down on the club. Shortening the shaft will prevent the club from taking too much sand and leaving the ball in the bunker. Hold the club face open through contact so that the face doesn't turn and become closed—and dig into the sand—as it comes toward the ball.

Ball below feet

The key here is to do what you have to do to stay balanced. That means taking a wider stance, about as wide as the width of your shoulders. But make sure your club will get down to the sand before the ball. Bend a little more than normal at your knees and concentrate on maintaining this posture throughout the stroke.

Desperation and the Putter

There is another option from the bunker, but I don't recommend it in all situations. In fact, I think you're much better off developing confidence with your sand wedge than resorting to your putter. But you can use it, if the circumstances are just right. Try the putter if you have . . .

. . . a good lie

. . . very smooth, firm (not fluffy) sand

. . . little or no lip on the bunker

. . . little or no rough between the edge of the bunker and the front of the green

. . . a pin that's cut close to the bunker

. . . water on the opposite side of the green (in play if you hit a bunker shot thin)

. . . no confidence in your sand wedge.

Now, I suppose I can see much of the logic in the first six of those conditions, but I can see no reason for not having confidence in your sand wedge. The club was invented specifically to make this particular situation easier. Take advantage of the club's benefits, take advantage of your ability to tailor your setup to the specific situation in the bunker, and you'll soon be able to take advantage of the sand instead of letting it take advantage of you.

How to Test the Sand

If you pay attention to the pros, you'll notice that fairly often they're pretty meticulous about getting their golf shoes into the proper position in the sand. One reason for doing this is fairly obvious: they want to establish a balanced position so they will be able to stay steady throughout their shot. But a second reason is especially important for the average player to pay attention to. When pros settle into a bunker, they're getting a sense of the consistency of the sand. You should, too.

By noticing what your feet are feeling as you get set up in the bunker, you'll know how you might have to adjust your swing or setup to better match the bunker conditions.

For instance, if your feet tend to sink into the sand and it feels fluffy, your club head will move through the sand with less effort and the ball will fly out of the bunker with

■ Strange Displays True Grit

Sometimes the best short-game shots aren't the ones that end up in the hole. Curtis Strange hit one of those vitally important short shots that lead to victory, and what's more, he may have put himself in the seemingly awkward position of having to hit a bunker shot on purpose. Bunkered on the final hole of regulation at the 1988 U.S. Open at the Country Club in Brookline, Massachusetts, Strange needed to get up and down from the deep sand trap fronting the final green to force an 18-hole playoff with his playing partner, Nick Faldo. After hitting a poor tee shot on the 18th hole, Strange actually may have hit his ball into the bunker on purpose. Years later he told reporters, "U.S. Open rough being what it is helped me make my decision that the bunker was not a bad place to be. And as it turned out, I had a very comfortable, slightly uphill lie to hit from." Of course, having a good lie and getting up and down in the intense pressure of the final hole of a U.S. Open are two different things. But Strange was up to the task, hitting his bunker shot to two feet, making the putt, and then going on to win the playoff comfortably the next day. Strange later said, "That bunker shot was the greatest shot I have hit in my life, there is no question about it."

a good deal of spin. Generally, you can get away with a slightly more open club face in this situation, but maintain your speed through the shot. You can also stand a little wider than normal and a little farther from the ball. This promotes a shallower angle of approach to the sand because of the arc of your swing, which will make it more likely that your sand wedge will glide through the sand and less likely that it will dig in and get stuck in the fluffy sand.

If, however, the sand feels firm, your swing probably will have to have a more vertical angle of attack. In other words, your swing will be more up-and-down into the sand instead of skimming across the top of the sand. To promote a more vertical swing, stand a little closer to the ball than normal and keep your weight more on your left side. The ball won't have as much spin from heavy sand, so expect your shots to roll a little more than usual. From especially heavy, firm sand, you might even consider using a 60-degree wedge that has no bounce angle. Firm conditions make it more likely that the club may skip through the sand, especially if, like the sand wedge, it has a substantial bounce angle.

Equipment Choices

As Gene Sarazen realized 70 years ago, and we all know today, the sand wedge may be the most important club you add to your set. Its ability to handle a variety of lies and distances, to say nothing of its obvious benefits in bunkers, will often make it your club of choice.

When selecting a sand wedge, consider the type of course you'll be playing regularly, the weight that feels comfortable to you, and the way a particular sand wedge fits in with the rest of your set. There are three important variables of sand wedges: degree of loft (from about 55 to 58 degrees), degree of bounce (eight degrees to 13 degrees), and swing weight (from D-1 to D-8). Remember, swing weight is simply a gauge of how heavy the club feels as you swing it. The higher the number, the more the weight feels concentrated in the head, as opposed to the grip.

If you play a variety of courses, it's best to stay within the middle range of specifications for loft and weight. However, if you play a course with hard sand and elevated greens, you should choose a more lofted wedge with little bounce and lighter weight. If you play a course with softer sand and heavier rough, you should choose a lower degree of loft in the range of 55 degrees, more bounce (about 10–12 degrees), and greater swing weight (D-5 and above).

If you're not sure of the specifications of the wedges you're looking at, ask your pro. If he doesn't know, contact the manufacturers. They'll be happy to provide you with all the information you need.

Drills

You can do a lot of different drills to improve your bunker technique, but nothing beats just climbing in the bunker and working on getting balls out of the bunker. Gary Player used to have a rule for bunker practice. He would not quit hitting bunker shots until he holed three shots. As the story goes, his wife had to bring his dinner out to the practice bunker one evening. Now, you don't have to start at that extreme, but certainly scattering a bag of shag balls in the bunker will get you into the habit of hitting successful bunker shots. When you hit a snag in your practice sessions, try some of these drills:

Split-grip drill

Separate your hands on the grip by about an inch and make bunker-shot swings. This will help keep your hands working together by encouraging a one-piece backswing. It will keep the club head and shaft in the center of your body as the club moves into the sand. This drill will help you correct the error of topping the ball in the bunker.

Stork drill

Make bunker swings while standing with 80 percent of your weight on your left foot. Drop your right foot behind your left and try to keep all but the toes of your right shoe off the ground. This will encourage your weight to stay forward throughout the shot. With your weight forward, you're more likely to swing down and through the sand instead of scooping at the bottom of your swing arc and having the club head dig into the sand.

Angled shaft drill

If you're taking too much sand and leaving your bunker shots short of the mark, make some practice swings by setting up with the shaft angled at about 18 inches outside the line the ball is on and about a foot behind the ball. This will produce a swing that is more around the body than up-and-down. With a shallower swing, the sand wedge should glide through the sand instead of burying itself in the sand well behind the ball.

Pre-set drill

In most instances, you have to make a full follow-through to execute a bunker shot properly. To do that, you have to get out of the habit of focusing on the ball during the swing and into the habit of focusing instead on the follow-through. Do this by turning your hips toward the target at address. Your body will naturally want to return to that position at the finish of your swing. Get ready to hit your shot, then just turn your hips to the target and hold this position for a count of two. Then, return to your normal address position and swing. This programming of the hip and torso turn will help you make a more complete and aggressive turn through your downswing, a must if you are going to get the ball out of the bunker.

CONCLUSION

▼ ▼ ▼ ▼

The Short Answer
to Lower Scores

Nobody hits the green in regulation every time. In fact, the best players in the world do it only slightly more than half the time. Most likely you aren't anywhere near that good. But that doesn't mean you can't score. As we have seen, your short game can be the most powerful part of your overall game. More than any other facet of your game, the short game can have the immediate effect of lowering your score, not just by saving you shots around the green but also by instilling a new level of confidence that permeates your entire approach to your round.

Like everything in golf, the challenge is to commit to developing that element of your game. Finding the time to practice is crucial to developing the ability to shoot scores that may be even better than your full swing shots might deserve. As the many examples of great short shots in the past have shown, you can strike the ball rather poorly or inaccurately and still find a way to neutralize or overcome those mistakes. With a solid short game, you can bring about a reversal of fortune that will have visible results every time you add up your score.

If the challenge of improving lies in practicing regularly, then the challenge of practicing regularly lies in making it interesting enough so that you will actually make time to do it. As Bobby Jones once wrote, "Practice must be interesting, even absorbing, if it is to be of any use." Using that sentiment as inspiration, I have devised a Short-Game Challenge. This little survival test is designed to put your skills around and on the greens to the test while at the same time firing up your sense of competition. I think this challenge mirrors the same sort of lasting emotions golf brings out in us in a full 18 holes. We not only are encouraged by our good results, but also at the same time see that bad results are easily correctable. If we find time to test our short game on a regular basis, we will hone those skills almost without really trying. That is why I urge you to take this test as often during the season as your time permits. The more you go through the test, the better your short game is going to get.

Remember, the shots around the greens are the most crucial to our score, and they're also potentially the most fun to practice. Hitting balls on the driving range at best can end up being monotonous and at its worst can end up ingraining bad habits in your full swing. In contrast, practicing your short-game shots almost always helps you improve. Why? Because the objective of any short-game shot is always much clearer than the vague objective of trying to make adjustments in your full swing. The objective is there right in front of you every time you hit a putt, chip, pitch, or bunker shot. The objective is getting the ball in the hole. The better you get at making the ball find its way into the hole, the more your scores are likely to improve. More succinctly, it's just as the great Bobby Jones once wrote: "To approach the hole remains the ultimate object in the game. Once the round is under way, the business in hand becomes that of getting results. Nothing else matters. . . .

"The secret of golf is to turn three shots into two."

The Short-Game Challenge

The Short-Game Challenge is a practice routine that, if followed faithfully, will lead to measurable improvement in your short game. The description of the Short-Game Challenge practice routine is followed by a chart outlining goals for players of various ability levels.

Part 1: Training Drills

Putting

1 Hit 10 three-foot putts in a row in a circle around the hole.

2 Hit 10 six-foot putts in a row.

3 Hit 10 10-foot putts in a row.

4 Hit 18 lag putts to six different holes at three different distances.

Chipping

1 With the nine-iron, chip to three different holes with three balls each hole. Record how often a chip shot finishes within a club length of the hole.

2 With the seven-iron, chip to three different holes with three balls to each hole.

3 With the five-iron, chip to three different holes with three balls to each.

Pitching

1 Hit 12 shots from four different spots around the green with a "good" lie. Record how often a pitch shot finishes within a club length of the hole.

2 Hit 12 shots from four different spots around the green with a "bad" lie.

3 Hit 12 shots, four each from 20, 40, and 60 yards in the fairway. Record how often each pitch shot finishes within the length of the flagstick from the hole.

Bunkers

Hit 12 shots, three each from five yards, 10 yards, and 15 yards. Record how often each sand shot finishes within two club lengths of the hole.

Short-Game Challenge Goals Chart

	PRO	LOW (0–9 handicap)	MID (10–19 handicap)	HIGH (20+ handicap)
PUTTING				
three-foot putt (out of 10)	10	8	7	6
six-foot putt (10)	7	5	4	3
10-foot putt (10)	4	3	2	1
18 lag putts (# of 3-putts)	0	1	2	6
CHIPPING				
nine-iron chip (9)	8	6	4	2
seven-iron chip (9)	7	6	3	2
five-iron chip (9)	6	5	3	2
PITCHING				
good-lie pitch (12)	8	7	5	3
bad-lie pitch (12)	6	4	3	1
20-yard pitch (12)	10	9	7	4
40-yard pitch (12)	9	7	5	3
60-yard pitch (12)	7	4	3	1
BUNKER SHOTS				
5-yard bunker shot (12)	10	8	5	2
10-yard bunker shot (12)	8	6	3	2
15-yard bunker shot (12)	7	5	2	1

Part 2: Combination Test

In this test your goal is to get the ball up and down. You have six different situations, three balls in each situation, 18 total.

Tour players average 39 strokes.

Low-handicap players average 42 strokes.

Mid-handicap players average 48 strokes.

Sand Wedge	2 Situations	Pitch Shots	Good Lie
Sand Wedge	2 Situations	Pitch Shots	Marginal Lie
Seven-iron	2 Situations	Chip and Run	Good Lie

Putt out after each situation.

About the Author

▼ ▼ ▼ ▼

Bill Moretti is director of instruction at the Academy of Golf Dynamics; he has served in this capacity for the past 20 years. The Academy of Golf Dynamics, located in Austin, Texas, is rated as one of the top 25 golf schools in the country by *Golf* magazine.

A Class-A PGA professional, Bill is known as one of the foremost authorities on the golf swing. *Golf* magazine and *Golf Digest* describe him as one of America's top 100 golf teachers. He has been honored by the Southern Texas PGA as Instructor of the Year. His effective teaching and communication techniques make him a popular speaker at national PGA conferences, a featured instructor on the Fox Sports Southwest Channel and the Golf Channel, and a regular contributor to *Golf* magazine, *Senior Golf* magazine, *Texas Golfer,* and *Gulf Coast Golfer.*

Bill's highly recognized teaching skills are continually sought out by PGA Tour professionals, including Fred Funk, J. L. Lewis, and Russ Cochran.